1920s Style

THIS IS A CARLTON BOOK

Published in 2013 by Carlton Books Limited
20 Mortimer Street
London W1T 3JW

10 9 8 7 6 5 4 3 2 1

Design © Carlton Books 2013
Text © Carlton Books, 2006, 2013, pages 7–11, 22–4, 138–
    144. Previously published in *Vintage Fashion* (2006).
Text © Caroline Cox, 2008, pages 14–15, 66–95, and 2010,
    pages 18–19, 118–137. Previously published in *Vintage
    Shoes* (2008) and *Vintage Jewellery* (2010).
Text © Marnie Fogg, 2009, pages, 16-17, 96–117 and 2010,
    pages 12-13, 42–65. Previously published in *Vintage
    Handbags* (2009) and *Vintage Fashion: Knitwear*
    (2010).

A CIP catalogue record for this book is available from the
British Library.

ISBN 978 1 78097 444 6

Special photography by Emma Wicks and Russell Porter
Design and illustrations by A&E Creative.

Printed in China

1920s Style

HOW TO GET THE LOOK OF THE DECADE

CAROLINE COX, MARNIE FOGG & KATE MULVEY

CARLTON
BOOKS

CONTENTS

Introduction: *Key Looks & Trends*

An evocative period that is revisited time and time again, the Roaring Twenties is often referred to as the "decade in which fashion entered the modern era". Released from the restrictive corset, women began enjoying a new athleticism. Soon sports such as swimming, cycling, golf and tennis became regular pastimes and clothing evolved to keep pace. Designers such as Coco Chanel and Elsa Schiaparelli championed trousers and sportswear for women, while Jean Patou began making two-piece suits and swimwear. The fashionable modern women of the 1920s, unlike their corseted Edwardian mothers, were active, unconventional and free.

One of the most enduring symbols of the decade is the flapper. A 'bright young thing' with bobbed hair and a short dress who drank, smoked, danced and aspired to a bohemian lifestyle, the flapper cultivated a skinny, boy-like figure with narrow hips and small breasts. The fundamental dress silhouette, labelled the 'garçonne', was a straight-line sleeveless shift with an elongated low-cut neckline. Unlike today, bras offered no support and were either camisoles or bandeaus. For bigger-breasted women, the side-lacer bra was worn, which could be pulled at the sides to flatten the breast and attain the essential minimal bustline. The waistline dropped to below the hip and eventually disappeared and the hemline rose to just below the knee. For the first time in centuries, women's legs were seen: the T-bar, Mary Jane, ankle strap and cut-away shoe all emphasized the once unseen ankle. Wealthier women wore heavily embellished silk – such as couture dresses by Edward Molyneaux in sequins, fringing and embroidery – while a new fabric, rayon, was available for those on more limited budgets. With the feel of silk, rayon provided the necessary slinkiness for parties and dancing, and by the late 1920s it was being used by Parisian fashion houses.

Silent-screen stars made a big impact in women's hair and makeup choices: Louis Brooks' bob haircut and Clara Bow's cupid lip were quickly copied, as was Theda Bara's kohl-rimmed eyes. The small handbag and vanity case contained the essential powder compact and lipstick. A close-fitting cloche hat enhanced the short hair styles, while the beaded cap was often worn for evening. The prevailing outerwear for the flapper was a shawl-collared wrapped coat, fastened on one side with a huge button or buckle, or fur – in full length for Hollywood glamour or as a wrap or stole. In *The British Fur Trade*, one writer estimated that two out of three women on any street in any town in England in the 1920s would be found wearing fur, if not as a coat, then as a trim.

Flapper style is sexy, adventurous, easy to move in and the ideal party look. High street stores regularly stock 1920s Art-Deco dresses and vintage stores can be plundered for authentic pieces. An overview of the decade's key trends in fashion, knitwear and accessories is given on the following pages, enabling you to re-create the Gatsby look easily and effectively or simply inspiring you to develop your own unique fashion sensibility.

Opposite Two luxurious fur-trimmed coats and one fur coat, circa 1922.

Right A model wearing a black panne velvet dress and cape trimmed with black fox fur, circa1925.

Fashion

Beading and fringing

Evening dresses with sequins, feathers and other ornate surface decorations were characteristic of the period, as in this fringed flapper dress seen here modelled by Joan Crawford in the 1920s. (1)

The sheath dress

The slinky sheath was made of chiffon, silk or crepe de chine, and clung to the female form from shoestring shoulder straps.

Geometrics

Sweeping bold curved patterns in deep colours that included dramatic red, black and blue appeared from 1910, along with other geometric patterns and Cubist motifs. (2)

Style Russe

Chanel's early 1920s Russian style, attributed to her liaison with Russian Grand Duke Dmitri, consisted of tunic shapes, fur trimmings and embroideries. This look reflected the influx of Russians to Paris after the Revolution. 'Style Russe' would be revisited by many designers to come, as in Saint Laurent's 'Russian Revolution' in the mid-1970s.

Bare backs and bias cuts

Cut on the bias, the new body-hugging dresses seemed to spiral round the body and moved with the wearer. Backless dresses, like this 1929 version, with or without trains, began to make an appearance later in the 1920s. (3)

1.

2.

3.

Dropped waist

Curves and the hourglass figure were out, and belts, sashes or ties were worn around the hips. The waist disappeared to create the fashionable beanpole look beloved in the 1920s, as typified in the illustration from Mab patterns, April 1925. (4)

4.

Le Garçonne look

A new androgyny accompanied the flapper era, and women wore short hair and dresses that were straight, loose and revealed bare arms. The lithe, athletic, modern form was the new sexy look.

Kimono style

Japanese-style dresses were seen as very exotic and heralded a new form of beauty based on simplicity and Oriental design. Many teagowns, like this 1925 dress, had the square-cut sleeves and shape of the kimono. (5)

5.

Sweaters

Silk or wool, and striped, plain or with trompe l'oeil motifs, the jumper was a key element in flapper style of the 1920s.

Trousers

'Bright young things' in the 1920s would wear silken pyjamas and sailor pants for early evening or as fashionable resort wear.

Velvets and furs

Fur coats, or coats trimmed in fur, were popular. Many had a single large button, or were wrapped over, a shawl collar, wide cuffs and fell to the knees. Velvet was also used in jackets, wraps and dresses; the sumptuous material was part of the style of opulence and the luxury of Art Deco fashion. (6)

6.

Knitwear

1.

Knitted jackets

An integral element of every woman's wardrobe, the knittted jackete had a relaxed silhouette that replaced the stiff tailoring of the tweed 'tailor-made' of the previous decade. This illustration dates from 1924: the long, loose shape, roll collar and single button placing the emphasis on the hip are typical of the period. (1)

Unstructured style

The demise of the corset led to flowing styles. Here a white silk knit-and-crochet dress for daywear dates from 1923. A crochet-edged boat neckline is teamed with a loosely draped fabric, structured by drawstrings at the waist. The silhouette of the open-sleeved tunic recalls the style worn for the fashionable 'callisthenics' exercises, for which participants adopted a version of classical Greek dress. (2)

2.

Beads and embroidery

Elaborate embellishment with embroidery and beadwork in Oriental and Art Deco motifs were a feature of knitwear design during this era, particularly for eveningwear. Ornate beadwork was also a feature of the decade's 'flapper dress', a short, sleeveless chemise.

Art Deco and geometrics

A 1925 oversized twinset designed by Joseph Paquin. Bold crochet-knitted, multicoloured chevron stripes are resonant of the influence of Art Deco. Both the seven-eighth-length coat and full-length dress have wide plain button bands from neck to knee. (3)

3.

The cardigan suit

This 1924 design by Jeanne Lanvin epitomizes the elegance and form of the outerwear of this period. The three-piece knitted suit of embellished long cardigan, narrow calf-length skirt and coordinated sweater was widely adopted at the beginning of the decade. (4)

4.

Sportswear influences

Golf fashions from 1927. The man's V-neck sweater and tie are mirrored by the woman's boyish striped sweater with large collar and tie; both wear polished brogues. Throughout the decade, hemlines rose and the knife-pleat skirt is knee-length. (5)

5.

Fair Isle patterns

Colourful hand-knit Fair Isle patterns exemplified the characteristic sportswear genre popularized by the Prince of Wales. The simple geometric motifs are essentially stocking stitch produced with more than one colour per row.

Knitted bathing suit

A hand-knitted bathing suit modelled in 1926. Although the knitted costume had an unfortunate tendency to sag and become waterlogged when worn, in the absence of elastic fibre only knitted structures provided the necessary fit and ease. (6)

6.

Shoes

Spectator shoes

A popular form of day shoe for the 1920s woman of fashion. Like male correspondent shoes, they came in two tones and were derived from the Oxford brogue. This pair is worn in the fashionable French resort of Deauville in 1923 with a simple linen drop-waisted dress. (1)

Metallic shoes

The fashion for metallics really took off in the 1920s as dancing cheek to cheek in nightclubs became de rigueur. Here, an evening bar shoe in silver kidskin is worn with a fur-trimmed wrap fashioned from a simple length of heavily embroidered fabric and an Egyptian influenced dress, circa 1928. (2)

Brocade and bars

Brocade, a heavy weight of woven fabric with an ornate raised design, was a popular fad. It was hard-wearing but maintained an air of luxury and was used in many a pair of bar-strap shoes. (3)

1.

2.

3.

The laced Oxford

The Oxford was low cut with an open or closed tab and three or more lace-holes. Originally derived from the men's Oxford, it was a popular day shoe. The lace-up women's Oxford, shown here with brogue detailing, has a high Cuban heel and arch to add femininity to a masculine style. This 1923 version would have made an excellent walking shoe. (4)

4.

The T-bar shoe

A pair of pretty pink-and-gold brocade T-bar shoes in a Cubist-derived Art Deco design, a popular leitmotif of the 1920s. During the middle of the decade strapwork on shoes became highly inventive and elaborate, involving a plethora of cut-out areas across the vamp and ankles. This pair is a rather more minimalist example of the look. (5)

5.

Mary Janes

Simple Mary Janes were standard footwear for the day and most women had at least one pair. This was a perfect shoe shape, being easy to walk in with the low heel and protectively high vamp.

Jewelled decoration

Ladies' evening shoes were highly decorative, with removable buckles and clasps as well as richly jewelled heels, often rendered in Art Deco designs. The heels become the focal point of the shoe and deliberately courted attention by directing the gaze up a pair of shapely ankles to the delights above. (6)

6.

Handbags

Matching accessories

The vogue for matching accessories to the outfit was a feature of 1920s fashion. This ensemble from 1929 was illustrated by Gordon Conway for *Tatler* magazine. The spring evening frock of figured chiffon is embroidered with the same design as the envelope-style evening bag and the satin slippers. (1)

1.

Small bags

Miniature hand-held purses and bags were a feature of the flapper style of the 1920s. Here a simple circular envelope style with small handles, dating from 1923, reflects the circular rings in contrasting colour appliquéd onto the sleeves of the coat. (2)

Metal mesh

The mesh bag reached the height of its popularity during the 1920s. This fine steel example is attached to a shaped copper alloy frame and trimmed with square-cut imitation sapphires. The single chain handle is constructed of rectangular links and the front has a geometric design in soft shades of copper and grey mesh. The base of the bag is trimmed with a dentate fringe. (3)

2.

3.

4.

Tango bags

The energetic and popular dances of the 1920s, such as the Charleston and the Tango, required a small bag that could either fit into the palm of the hand or wrap around the wrist so the bag was secure during the exertions of the dance. This finely corded version has a gilt metal frame, a snap closure and a handle of matching black silk. The bag is gathered at the base into a silk-covered button. (4)

Tapestry and embroidery

Embroidered and needleworked bags featured florals and landscape scenes. Here an embroidered bag with an embellished clasp detracts from the severity of the outfit on the left, lending a feminine note to the strict tailoring. 'Tailor-mades', such as the suits here made in 1926 by Augstabernard, were worn for country pursuits and a feature of most women's wardrobes. (5)

Geometrics and Art Deco

Influences from ancient civilizations in the form of geometric stepped designs, chevrons and sunray patterns became stylized decorative features. Here a rectangular beaded evening bag dating from the 1920s is constructed from black and metallic glass beads worked into a Greek key pattern. (6)

5.

6.

Jewellery

Venetian beads

Beads enjoyed a vogue as they could be produced in a variety of vivid colours and intricate designs. Venetian beads incorporated floral features that today are prized by collectors all over the world. They are created by heating and stretching glass rods, which are then thinly sliced and moulded into beads. (1)

1.

Bangles and cuff bracelets

Silent-screen star Olga Baclanova, aka the 'Russian Tigress', models the cuff bracelet, a popular jewellery design in the 1920s. The cuff could be simple when moulded in Perspex; avant-garde and 'barbaric' when sported in armfuls; or the height of luxury when fashioned out of gold and studded with diamonds. (2)

Art Deco

Many women wore fan-shaped Spanish-style hair combs as not everyone had a bob in the 1920s. The fan, together with the chevron, was one of the most popular motifs of this period and appears in architecture and interiors as well as jewellery designs. This celluloid comb from the mid-1920s is outlined in blue rhinestones. (3)

2.

Egyptian and ethnic motifs

Inspiration came from Oriental, Indian and Egyptian art. Following Howard Carter's discovery of Tutankhamen's tomb and artefacts in 1922, Egyptian motifs became all the rage.

3.

Tasselled necklaces

Long necklaces made of glass beads and ending in a tassel, originally called sautoirs, were re-named 'flapper beads'. They were accompanied by tassel earrings that dangled below newly shorn bobbed hair, and tasselled shimmy dresses that created an energetic sense of movement when participating in new dance crazes like the Charleston. (4)

Machine-cut gemstones

High-quality cutting and polishing with the aid of machines took over from the traditional hand work. This meant that more facets and complicated new cuts could be introduced. Plastic also suited the new mechanical processes and was available in a wide variety of colours and finishes.

4.

Geometric settings

Edwardian floral designs seemed desperately outmoded to a new generation of young women who were forging ahead to find their place in a modern post-war world. The garçonne look of the 1920s needed a new kind of jewellery to match. Geometric settings held sway, as in this diadem and collar by Cartier from 1926. (5)

Glass and crystal

Glass and crystal combined with silver was a combination that could achieve sparkling effects when matched with beaded flapper dresses. Here a silver necklace is given a visual lift with the insertion of carved red glass tablets. (6)

5.

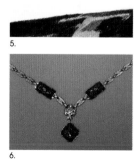

6.

Beaux-Arts des Modes

Flapper Fashions

At the turn of the century, the Edwardian sun shone for a privileged few. Fashion was dictated from the top and the decorative female in her frills and flounces seemed to waft through society while caged in an ironclad corset. As modernism gathered pace, both the corset and the suffocating Victorian values of the time were torn apart, and in 1909 a new linear silhouette came into fashion. Societal norms were challenged, and an explosion of originality and progressive ideas in art, film, psychology and the role of women were established.

Ethnic elements – Oriental themes, ancient Greece and Japanese prints – all influenced fashion, shown in exotic-styled motifs, the natural form and the curvilinear designs of the avant-garde. Added to this, following the tragedy of the First World War and post-1918 fashion, women went wild. Hemlines went up, waistlines went down and flappers boogied to the Charleston, the Bunny Hop and the new hot sound of jazz. Fringes, beads and tassels ornamented short dresses worn above the knee and the accent was on youth and 'misbehaving'.

By the 1920s the media age was beginning. People acquired their sartorial ideas not from their 'betters' but from listening to the radio, copying stars in the cinema and reading about the fashions in *Vogue* and *Vanity Fair*. The growing popularity of sports such as tennis and cycling prompted a new and simpler look. Jean Patou, Madeleine Vionnet and Coco Chanel were among the designers who created the first modern style for women still seen today.

Modernism & Geometrics

'God the machine' was the mantra of the Modernist age. The turn of the century brought the automobile, the steam ship and the aeroplane. These were all innovations that had a tangible effect not only on the choice of fabrics, design and colours used, but also on the easy-to-wear fashions of the time. Designers created styles that catered to the cosmopolitan woman – 'Shipboard smartness' and 'Riviera chic', as *Vogue* dubbed them in 1926.

The flat, straight-up-and-down dresses of the 1920s were perfect for the stylized geometric-patterned prints that defined the Modernist period. Influenced by the Cubist and Futurist art movements, their dynamic, uneven designs, straight lines, spirals, cones and zig-zags were all incorporated into the fashions of the day. Cubist abstract motifs were sewn on to dresses and evening coats. Horizontal stripes were juxtaposed with triangles on dresses, with the same pattern lining the coat. Embroidered circles and triangles in silver and gold thread brought to life the popular black evening dresses of the day, and diagonal patterns with shadings from black to grey produced amazing graphic designs from the prevailing Art Deco style.

Jean Patou's famous sweaters, with their Cubist-style blocks of contrasting colour in horizontal stripes inspired by the paintings of Picasso and Braque, were worn by the beau monde. Cubist pieces were all the rage, as were Egyptian-style motifs, with serpent designs, hieroglyphics and scarabs either appliquéd or embroidered on to day and evening dresses.

The Modernist designers often concentrated on purifying form and cut: Vionnet, Lanvin and Chanel controlled the amount of ornamentation they used and, like the Cubists, were more interested in form and design than embellishment. Lucien Lelong's Ligne kynetique was a range of severely tailored cloth dresses in two shades of jersey with a pared-down simple shape that suggested movement in the design.

Pleats and tucks were often executed as designs in themselves. Treated geometrically, there were perpendicular tucks in all directions – suits with horizontal pleats on the bodice and vertical pleating on the skirt were popular and contributed to the Modernist rectangular look.

Right Silk white-and-navy dress with triangle detailing from the 1920s exhibits the fascination with clean Modernist geometry.

Colour palette

Contrasting colours in the bold palette of the Fauvist painters were characteristic of the Modernist look. Black and white was one of the smartest of colour schemes, and part of the avante-garde that dominated fashion at that time introduced neutral grey and beige. Other colour combinations – red and green; black, red and orange; and acid green and cerise pink – were popular Art Deco colours. Black was often used as a background for bright motifs – black taffeta dresses with red, green and mauve embroidery on collars and circular panels of embroidery on the skirt, for example. Contrasting hues of different browns and greys on a black background gave clothes a graphic look.

Right and below A late 1920s silk serpentine-print dress. Although it is by an unknown designer, the graphic interlocking snake-like print and sharp curved lines that drape the form clearly reference Modernism. Note the asymmetrical draped collar and the buttoned-waist detail.

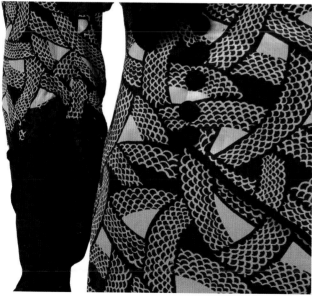

15

GASTON DROUET, Editeur
6, Rue Ventadour, PARIS

n.98

Création Redfern
portée par Mᵐᵉ Cora Laparcerie.

Paris Élegant

Reproduction interdite

Pl. 115

Supplément au N° 134 - 1920

Opposite A black and grey patterned silk evening dress with a sash of black silk by Redfern. *Paris Élégant,* 1920.

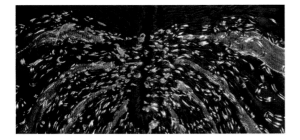

Above, below and right Black 1920s Paquin dress with pink embroidery. Paquin's signature colour was pink but she was also known for her dramatic use of black. Deep slits on the bodice and the back sleeves, a handkerchief hem, and vertical ruching at the waist mark some of the unique details on this rare piece. There would have been a ribbon threaded through on the back.

Fabrics and Decoration

The decorative arts and fashion fused during the 1920s to usher in a flamboyant look, and the simplicity of the cut and shape of the times was offset by elaborate surface decoration.

Technical developments within the textile industry meant that new fabrics were being created, and mass-produced rayon dresses with the appearance of silk were popular for both daywear and eveningwear. Meyer artificial silks and woollens – Pelgram & Meyer was one of the pioneer silk mills in early twentieth-century America – were available in a variety of weaves, colours and textures.

During the day, women would wear angular styles in practical materials like jersey, silk twill, mohair, kasha and rayon. Dresses in coarsely woven silk, jersey cardigans, lightweight tweeds and handwoven brocades were considered chic.

Fluttery evening frocks in flimsy materials like crepe satin and crepe georgette shimmered with diamanté. Dresses using the shiny side of the satin for the trimming and the dull side for the body section could be seen everywhere, and silk in combination with cotton was worn. Silver, gold and coloured laces were often combined with satin, lamé, taffeta, crepe de chine and georgette. Sumptuous lamé gowns of green and gold, worn with pearls and overlaid with thin lace, shone in the night, as did acid-green moiré tubular frocks. Mariano Fortuny's hand-stencilled velvet coats and dresses woven with shimmering metallic thread were inspired by sixteenth-century velvets and his motifs and patterns reflected paintings of that period.

Surface decoration and trimmings

The tubular-shaped dresses of the day were an ideal surface for embroidery and other decoration. Appliqué, flocking, raised cord, metal and coloured thread, particularly gold and silver, were all seen in dresses following Art Deco styles. Silver embroidery livened up black chiffon dresses and embroidered bands were used to trim décolleté and bolero tops.

Paquin's gowns of green chiffon embroidered with pearls and gold threads on a Chinese design, with bands of embroidery forming the dropped waist, were seen on the pages of *Vogue*. Embroidery silks added glamour and diamanté embroidery for evening was said to be so 'brilliant' that the nightclubs hardly needed lighting. Beads were embroidered – creating motifs, lines or trimmings – on most eveningwear.

Oriental, Cubist and floral appliqué provided a decorative surface design technique, and gold and silver leather appliqué added dimension and texture to the background fabric. The beaded evening dress of the 'Roaring '20s' is the signature vintage garment.

Opposite above
Sequins, beads and appliqué on a skirt from the 1920s. Sequins at this time were sometimes made of wax, and easily melted. In gowns you may find deterioration of the sequins where a dancing partner's hands would rest.

Opposite, below left
A 1928 Vionnet garment decorated with a stylized rose by the design house Lesage. Masterful shading is achieved by strategic use of subtly different colours. Lesage has been creating haute couture embroidery since 1924, and many designers have built a piece or a collection around a Lesage motif.

Opposite, below right
Ornate beadwork and with lace and flower appliqué on a satin bridal gown, 1905.

Designed to be 'brilliant', some dresses were completely covered in brightly coloured glass beads or genuine gems such as crystal and jet: black beads made from coral or glass. These could be sewn on to lightweight silk, rayon, crepe or chiffon to create a striking look.

White crepe georgette dresses with diamanté beads and pailettes were common. Black chiffon dresses with silver and gold beads were particularly spectacular, and whole skirts edged with crystal beads in the same colour or edged with rhinestone embroidery sparkled. The craze for sequins was a hallmark of the decade, as they reflected the light and could be overlapped to produce linear patterns.

Dresses were as diverse as everything else. White crepe de chine frocks were fringed with chatelaine and dresses with three-tiered fringing, the top layer of the fringe outlining the bolero top, created a swaying flounced shape. Wide fringed scarves were worn to give extra motion to the silhouette. Feathers were attached to the bodices and skirts of dresses and even featured as headgear.

Further ornamentation was evident in ruffles, sewn in even tiers and along the edges of skirts and jumpers. Bows were worn at the neck, hip and down the front and back of dresses, and lingerie touches at the neck and sleeves were popular. Leather – sometimes metallized – and fur trimmings on cuffs, collars and hems were key details. But for the ultra-glam woman, fur-lined and fur-trimmed gold lamé coats were a must.

Notable designers

Certain couturiers and designers of the period were notable for their expertise, not only in design but also for their use of embellishment. Known for her spectacular beading techniques and innovative surface embellishment, Lanvin introduced free-flowing ribbons at the neck or hip of the dress, petals and ruffles and delicate appliqué in pastel colours – especially Lanvin blue – and her elaborate thread embroideries were inspired by exotic travel and other elements.

Callot Soeurs' dresses in embroidered satin or velvet with Eastern motifs in kingfisher blue and black with gold and copper highlights were worn by society gals, as were their silver and gold lamé evening dresses and decorative dragon and paisley medallion motifs. The sisters – Marie, Marthe, Regina and Joséphine, who formed the house in 1895 and who were authorities on antique lace – combined unusual materials such as rubberized gabardine or calf skin with gossamer silks worked with bands of gold lace or silk flowers.

Artist-designer Mary Monaci Galenga's Moyen Age teagown with a square or V-neck and tabard was a must-have of the time. Made of silk velvet or crepe de chine, the gown had panels of floating chiffon set into the side seams and was strewn with large Venetian glass millefiori beads. It also featured gold or silver stencilling in different tones and a variety of patterns.

Above Fortuny seashell-stencil turquoise velvet, 1920s. The designer's stencilled velvets have the look of antique frescoes, with multiple layers of pigment.

Right A red silk cashmere party dress with a large skirt sash tied at the back as a large loop. *Dernières Créations,* circa 1923.

Opposite Mary Monaci Galenga stencilled crimson velvet, 1920s. Born in 1880, Galenga was a mentor of the Italian Futurists and developed the technique of stencilling gold onto velvet. A contemporary of Fortuny, by 1914 she was making clothes and textiles. Both Fortuny and Galenga were known for their Renaissance revival designs.

Above Ladies 1920s
daywear with dropped-waist
dresses and pleated skirts
with jackets, worn with
cloche hats. The hemlines are
high at just below the knee.

New Silhouettes

The fashions of the 1910s are the sartorial missing link between the *belle époque* (1890–1914) and the modern fashion of the 1920s. The Edwardian S-bend silhouette made way for the less restrictive empire line with raised waist (1908), followed by the dropped waist (1920s), where the waist and bosom simply disappeared.

The empire line and the hobble

By 1908 societal mores were beginning to relax and this could be seen in the changing silhouette of women's fashions. When Paul Poiret introduced his empire line in that same year, it was greeted with great enthusiasm. Characterized by the columnar silhouette and a slim skirt, his empire-style dresses were unprecedented. The waistline crept up from the waist to below the bosom, and the hemline rose slightly accordingly. With the waist no longer the focal point, the dresses were suspended from the shoulders, creating a linear form.

Loosely cut sleeves with crossed bodices were seen in evening dresses and the evening coats were based on simple wraps with batwing sleeves. These garments then became working surfaces, which the designers could use for their increasingly opulent styles. Fur trimmings were very popular and served as the new status symbol.

Couturier Jacques Doucet's empire dresses were made of airy fabrics and had intricate floral details showing the influence of Art Nouveau's decorative language. Free-flowing with a simple construction, they were made in one piece and fell straight down, which respected instead of bifurcated the natural form.

Paul Poiret introduced the hobble skirt in 1910 – a return to female imprisonment, as women's legs were clamped together in a skirt that was unfeasibly narrow from the knees to the ankles, causing women to walk like Japanese geishas. Yet it proved to be a short-lived trend – 'freedom' was the new buzz word.

The wartime crinoline

The long, clinging high-waisted dresses were swept away during the First World War when the chemise dress appeared. Pioneered by Lanvin, Worth and Paquin, the chemise was cut loose and full and was belted under the bosom. Skirts rose suddenly to just above the ankle and filled out. More romantic in style, these new skirts were flared, and although they had layers of petticoats underneath – sometimes to crinoline proportions – they were easy to walk in.

The bodices of dresses were unfitted and the bust was flat. Women started to wear open-necked blouses that combined fashion and function, as everything was now loose and biased towards freedom of movement. They were simple and elegant, made in velvets for the afternoon and Charles Worth's tinted tulles and muslins for the evening.

There was a brief return to the barrel skirt in 1917 by couturiers such as Callot Soeurs, Doeuillet and Paquin. Cut wide over the hip, it had the pannier look – pulling the dress out at the hips – of a bygone age, sometimes with two or three gathered tiers.

Postwar fashions

After the war, fashion did not quite know what direction it should take. The greater freedom women had enjoyed meant that fashion could not go backwards. Easy-to-wear elegance became the order of the day, although for the first half of the 1920s sudden changes of line or length of skirt were usual, and the hemline rose and fell in an erratic manner.

Coco Chanel and Jean Patou championed the shorter length with their forward-looking jersey suits and sporty style. Although in 1919 the hemline rose again and the look of the '20s flapper was nascent, most women still wore widish peg-top skirts and A-line styles – only slightly shorter than before. Jeanne Lanvin's new fluffed-up crinolines were the exception to the slimmer silhouette.

In 1920 an unprecedented mid-calf hemline came in at 7.5 cm (3 in) above the ankle and with dresses high-waisted. However, twelve months later, hemlines dropped again, practically to the ankle. The longer skirts were circular in cut, and dresses and tops were loosely belted to just below the natural waistline and above the hip. Eveningwear was still elaborately trimmed, with fringing all the rage.

From 1922 to 1924 hemlines were 10–13 cm (4–5 in) from the ankle and the focus was on a vertical silhouette – this was achieved by dropping the waistline dramatically to the hip and by vertically striped tunics or vertical pleats and tucks.

The two-piece came into fashion. This consisted of a blouse or jumper and skirt combination, the top completely unfitted and worn over the skirt to just below hip level, sometimes with a wide belt or sash. Along with ensemble dresses, which consisted of a matched dress and jacket, these were strong fashions, lasting throughout the 1920s. The bateau neckline – slashed straight from one shoulder to the other – was popular, as were scooped necks, V-necks, sailor collars and three-quarter-length sleeves.

'Paris agrees to disagree about the length of skirts,' said *Vogue* in 1923, as designers could not make up their mind about how much leg to show. Some women loved Chanel's shorter skirt – a radical 22–25 cm (9–10 in) off the ground; others preferred Edward Molyneux's longer Egyptian sheaths that were almost ankle length.

Opposite left and right
Beaded gold and cream straight-line 1926 flapper dress, without and with the cardigan. The geometric diamond design is classic Art Deco. The neckline is a V-neck with fill-in and the irregular hem falls to the knees, typical of the period.

The Age of the Flapper

By 1924 the wise-cracking flappers were as much known for their reckless behaviour as for their style. Smoking and putting their make-up on in public, the bright young things drank and danced the Shimmy and the Bunny Hop in a frenzy of excitement. Taping up their breasts to get rid of unwanted curves, they looked youthful and boyish, and the new silhouette was slender, straight up and down like a board, and in fact became known as 'le garçonne'.

As if to herald the new mood, the waistline dropped dramatically in 1925 to below the hip, and by 1927 it had disappeared altogether and the hemline risen a scandalous 38 cm (15 in) to just below the knee. The flapper look was at its apogee and extremely short skirts were worn day and night. But hemlines crashed down along with Wall Street in 1929, just as waistlines and busts edged their way into fashion consciousness.

Flapper dresses were straight, loose and sleeveless, revealing a new body awareness. Arms were bare, and legs and backs were exposed for the first time, becoming new erogenous zones. The illusion of nudity was heightened by the use of diaphanous fabrics and little adornment. Beading was used to emphasize the see-through materials and catch the light, yet also highlighted the risqué nature of the outfits.

The short shift dress, which fell straight down from the shoulders and stopped above the knees, dominated the mid- to late 1920s. Ornamented with geometric and abstract designs, the chemise was often beaded with bands of glittering sequins.

For daywear the three-piece jersey suit was the cornerstone of female fashion: a blouse worn with a patterned or plain knitted sweater or a Chanel-style cardigan jacket with pockets was teamed with a narrow, short, pleated skirt. Day dresses were simple or decorated with details such as horizontal tucks, seaming or bias-cut panels and square boatnecks.

Opposite and below
Molyneux orange silk 1925 dress with silver and gold embroidery. Even on flapper dresses Molyneux's designs were more minimalist than those of his contemporaries – robust fabrics, strong Modernist motifs and a perfect cut made them demanding though utterly elegant pieces.

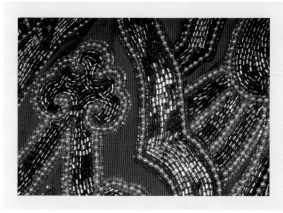

Signature flapper elements

- Uneven split hems and handkerchief points that are longer at the back
- Egyptian- and Art-Deco-inspired motifs
- Visible seam decoration and double seams
- Diagonal lines and asymmetric trimmed necklines
- Pockets, buttons and belts
- Pleated panels on skirts and knife pleats
- Day dresses belted around the hips
- Low-cut necks and backs, with thin straps
- Narrow trailing scarves, sometimes attached to dresses

Combinations of fabrics were used and two-tones, graded shades were popular, as were mannish suits, ties and small geometric prints.

A pioneer with Coco Chanel of the 'garçonne' look, Jean Patou designed sports ensembles with gradating stripes that could be worn with his geometric jumpers and cardigans on the Riviera. He designed beige three-piece jersey suits, dresses and wraps. His afternoon flapper-style crepe dresses had self-tied shoulder bows or decorative seams worked in zig-zags.

The bright young things wore trousers at home in the early evenings or at the beach. Loosely cut with drawstring or elasticated waists, they were sometimes called Oxford bags and fastened at the side for modesty. Paquin's Chinese-printed satin pyjamas with embroidered satin jacket were all the rage.

The perfectly straight-line collarless coat that buttoned at the waist like a cardigan jacket and a high-collar coat with a sash at the waist maintained their popularity, as did the slightly circular coat with fur collar that wrapped over on the diagonal, fastening with a single loop and button at hip level.

Eveningwear

The modern social whirl of cabarets, fancy dress parties and dancing gave rise to more extravagant eveningwear. By 1928 Paris was determined to abandon the tubular dresses, and floating panels and Vionnet's bias-cut dresses, which followed the contours of the body, became popular. Draperies from the hips gave the illusion of length and fullness, and movement was added with attached panels or uneven hemlines. Chanel's black evening dresses with huge transparent draperies, Paquin's acid-green moiré dresses with a V-neck and bulk at the hip, and Molyneux's transparent printed dresses with full, scalloped skirts and arm draperies are all significant flapper styles.

Crystal-beaded waves with coral fish and lilac flamingos in lotus ponds were some of Molyneux's unconventional surface decoration on flapper dresses. He experimented with ostrich feathers and buttons resembling cigarette butts or lipsticks, and his beaded chemises are some of the most exquisite.

Opposite A fashionable dress by Erté worn with a long string of beads.

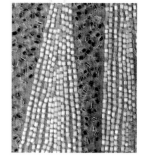

Top Silver lamé flower-patterned Erté-style dress with a flower corsage at the waist, early 1920s.

Above right and right Cream and white 1925 beaded flapper dress in starburst Art Deco design.

Knitwear & Sportswear

Opposite Coco Chanel exudes modernity in 1929. She wears a float-jacquard knit two-piece cardigan suit over a striped sweater with strands of pearls: components that formed the basis of the signature style that was to remain until her death in 1971.

The radically simpler clothes of the 1920s introduced a fashionable body shape of svelte serpentine slimness based on the chemise, a straight low-waisted dress that hung from the shoulder and grew ever shorter as the decade progressed. This shortened skirt created a new erogenous zone, the legs, and kickstarted the global hosiery industry. Previously knitted on a circular machine and only steamed into shape, so that with wear they bagged at the knee and ankle, stockings now began to be fully fashioned. Made in two pieces and sewn together, knitted in beige or flesh-toned silk, the legs appeared thrillingly naked.

The newly tanned and worked-out body, fresh from the tennis court or ski slope, embraced this new near-nudity. The Modern movement demanded the pursuit of the perfect form and this included not only streamlining products and architecture, but also women's bodies. Hips and breasts were out of fashion; the garçonne silhouette perfectly suited a relaxed way of dressing that didn't differentiate significantly between active sportswear and daywear, particularly in America. The loose flowing lines of the chemise appealed to the 'flapper', a phenomenon of the decade, a notoriously free-spirited, young woman leading a hedonistic lifestyle supposedly predicated on high living and loose morals. In 1922 US magazine *Outlook* printed an article by Ellen Welles Page, a self-confessed flapper:

> I wear bobbed hair, the badge of flapperhood. I powder my nose.
> I wear fringed skirts and bright colored sweaters…
> I adore to dance. I spend a large amount of time in automobiles.
> I attend hops and proms; and ballgames and crew races, and
> other affairs at men's colleges…

Informal Dressing

The new androgyny of silhouette resulted in the diminishing influence of the great Parisian couturiers such as Drecoll and Jacques Doucet, and even Paul Poiret found himself out of step with the aesthetic of the time.

Although Coco Chanel opened her salon in 1916, it was during this decade that she proved most iconoclastic and influential. In 1923 she met the Duke of Westminster, whose name was rarely mentioned without the soubriquet 'the richest man in England'. During their relationship Chanel purloined items of his sporting dress, sequestering tweed jackets, trousers and hand-knitted hip-length cardigans with roomy pockets, worn with hand-knit beige stockings.

This aesthetic translated in the summer to clothes that allowed for the new athleticism – tennis, golf, swimming and horse-riding. Ironically, the leisure clothes of the aristocracy rendered fashion newly democratic. Three-piece cardigan suits did not require a ladies maid to dress the wearer; they were easy to manufacture and easy to copy. Speed was central to the age, mass production increased, and the fashion industry geared up to provide the new women consumers with their needs.

The informal way of dressing complied with the American fashion notion of comfort and ease. Although Parisian imports and Parisian copies made up the majority of high fashion in the prestigious department stores at the beginning of the decade, the proportion of American fashion in the shops had changed dramatically by the decade's end. New York designers such as Berthe Holley pioneered the concept of separates; a collection of interchangeable pieces comprising sweaters, blouses and skirts and the ever-popular cardigan jacket.

Chanel's jersey suits and beige tricot dresses were successful imports, as were Elsa Schiaparelli's trompe l'oeil sweaters and Jean Patou's golf ensembles. All the European designers understood the need to appeal to the American market, Patou going so far as to hire American models for his Parisian fashion shows. Knitwear included luxurious sports clothes such as angora cardigans and cashmere jersey ensembles by design houses such as Kurzman, whose exotic emporium, built from European castles, was sited on New York's Fifth Avenue.

Below and opposite above left Mustard, cream and brown chevron-striped and belted tunic in racked half-cardigan stitch. The elongated shape is formed by the 'cut and sew' method, with the hem and cuffs sewn by hand. A rectangular tortoiseshell buckle continues the geometric theme.

Opposite above right and opposite below Attributed to Chanel, this long loose cardigan with matching sweater uses a four-colour stripe to create an undulating surface of light and shade. An early version of the twinset, it is produced by the 'cut and sew' method, including a curious series of small dart suppressions at the nape of the neck.

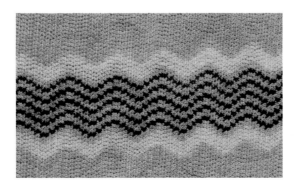

This page The geometric patterning of these three-piece cardigan suits dating from 1928 reflects the influence of the Art Deco movement. Use of broad striped trims to create decorative revers reinforces the architectural detailing produced by the striped cuffs and pocket edges.

Art Deco and Cubism

A generation of women brought up to provide garments for the armed forces during the First World War carried on knitting throughout the following decade, now using their skills to produce fashionable jumpers rather than serviceable socks. It was a decade dominated by youth and the 'Bright Young Things'.

The hemline rose to unprecedented heights, freeing the body for the dance revolution of ragtime and jazz. In 1922 a leaflet by Weldon, publisher of *Practical Needlework*, featured patterns for 'jazz jumpers', highly patterned and brightly coloured hand-knits that reflected the artistic preoccupations of the time, including the trapezoidal, zig-zagged, geometric shapes, and the bold use of stepped forms and sweeping curves of Art Deco.

Art Deco originated in Paris, where it was called the Moderne, with the *Exposition Internationale des Arts Décoratifs et Industriels Modernes* (International Exposition of Modern Industrial and Decorative Art), although there had been some indications of the fragmented style before then. Paris, keen to promote itself as the global capital of luxury and style, was witness to the birth of a glittering and glamorous design movement that was to dominate decorative design over the next two decades. The movement peaked in popularity in Europe during the 1920s, but continued in the United States throughout the 1930s. It was inspired by various sources, including Constructivism, Cubism, Modernism, Futurism and the 'primitive' arts of Africa, ancient Egypt and Mayan designs from Central America expressed in fractionated, crystalline, faceted forms.

The very nature of knitted fabric – its innate structure of horizontals and verticals – allowed for the geometric exploitation of colour and flat planes and angles inspired by Cubism. Jean Patou produced jumpers featuring blocks of contrasting colour and horizontal stripes inspired by the work of Pablo Picasso and Georges Braque. At the same time as Cubist works were being shown in Paris, artists Robert and Sonia Delaunay were experimenting with colour in art and design, investigating a process called *simultanéisme*; simultaneous design occurs when one colour is placed next to another, and then 'mixed' by the eye. Sonia's first large-scale painting in this style was *Bal Bullier* (1912–13). Increasingly intrigued by the application of these principles to design, she extended her practice to include stage sets, furniture, fabrics, wall coverings and clothing. In 1924 she opened a fashion studio with couturier Jacques Heim; together they created a sensation with their Boutique Simultanée.

Above and below

A 'cut and sew' sweater in black and white jersey, banded with solid black knitted straps to match the asymmetrical neckline: the diamond effect was produced by laddering back the face loops of 'normal' rib jacquard jersey.

Opposite A formal kimono-style jacket evokes Oriental brocades with its stylized Art Deco florals. Two-colour, striped back-rib jacquard forms the fabric structure – the same structure as demonstrated in the garment on page 47, before it has been laddered.

This page A knitted and embroidered jacket in black rayon or 'art silk'. Sumptuous beadwork in Chinese red bugle beads and metallic spheres lavishly borders every panel, recalling Oriental sources rendered into Art Deco motifs. The pattern is worked in a 'vermicelli' cursive line.

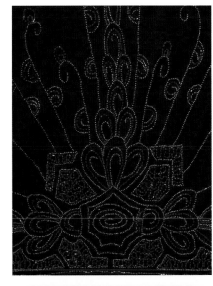

Far left Chinoiserie and other 'Orientalist' themes were a popular subject for the embroidered embellishment that lent itself to the vogue for bohemian dress, an exotic element of 1920s fashion. Here a black rayon-knit tunic dress has a contrasting panel of burnt orange. Throughout the garment, the bird and flower patterns are rendered by hand in crewelwork.

Left In contrast, this similarly-styled knitted tunic dress is embroidered in an all-over repeat pattern of roses using a mechanical Schiffli embroidery machine. The large-scale industrial machine employs a form of pantograph mechanism to simultaneously sew cursive stitching in repeat along a length of fabric.

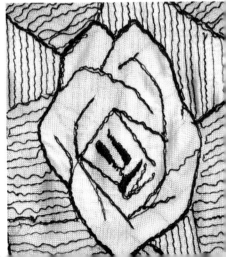

This page An 'Ottoman' semi-tailored jacket in cream rayon jersey. The opulence of the all-over embroidery, resonant of the floriated abstractions of Scottish designer Charles Rennie Mackintosh, renders the work as rich as a woven brocade. The use of Bakelite buckles at the waist and cuffs affirms the contemporary interest in this material.

Anyone for Tennis?

The exhilaration of being at peace sent the affluent classes into a whirl of sporting activity following the First World War. Polo, sailing, horse-racing and tennis became international events.

'Sport has more to do than anything else with the evolution of the modern mode,' said British *Vogue* in 1926, 'there is only one thing of which everyone is convinced… and that is the perfection of adaption to the needs of a game which modern dress has evolved.'

Opportunist manufacturers, aware of the marketing potential, exploited the market accordingly. New brand names like Superga, Dunlop and Slazenger supplied improved performance-wear, while luxury labels such as Louis Vuitton supplied the tennis kits and Hermès the racket covers. René Lacoste, the French seven-time Grand Slam tennis champion, decided that the stiff tennis attire then worn was too cumbersome and uncomfortable for optimum performance on the court. He designed a white, short-sleeved, loosely knit piqué cotton (he called the cotton fabric *jersey petit piqué*) shirt with an unstarched, flat protruding collar, a buttoned placket, and a longer shirttail in back than in front (known today as a 'tennis tail'), which he first wore at the 1926 US Open championship.

In 1927 Lacoste placed a crocodile emblem on the left breast of his shirts, as the American press had begun to refer to him as 'the Alligator' owing to his aggressive style of playing. Its sartorial rival, the polo shirt, was created in 1920 by Lewis Lacey, an Argentine Irish haberdasher and polo player. He produced a shirt that was embroidered with the logo of a polo player, a design originating at the Hurlingham Polo Club near Buenos Aires. The term 'polo shirt', which previously referred only to the long-sleeved, buttoned-down shirts traditionally used in polo, soon became a universal name for the tennis shirt.

Tennis fashion for women included knitted sleeveless pullovers with ribbed welts in contrasting colours, the forerunner of the classic tennis and cricket sweater with its striped V-neck. The female body was now celebrated for its athleticism, and sporting heroines such as Suzanne Lenglen, known as the 'Divine Lenglen', were the feminine ideal. A symbol of emancipation, Lenglen was as renowned for her fashionability as for her prowess on the court. The couturier Jean Patou was commissioned to design a pleated knee-length skirt and a sleeveless cardigan for her, and eventually he went on to establish a sportswear department in 1922, alongside couturiers such as Jeanne Lanvin and Jacques Heim.

Above Daringly baring her arms in 1925, French tennis player Suzanne Lenglen helps set the trend for the new female archetype of fashionable athleticism. Her coordinated signature headband accessorizes the tunic dress and long, sleeveless knitted gilet.

Opposite above A wool, plain-knit undervest with shoelace straps and a drawstring top by knitwear manufacturer John Smedley from the 1920s.

Opposite below As fashion became more form-friendly throughout the following decade, underwear reflected a greater body consciousness, seen here in a fine wool vest by John Smedley with fully-fashioned bra top from the 1930s.

John Smedley and the Isis Shirt

The 1920s heralded the production of British knitwear manufacturer John Smedley's most iconic garment, the Isis tennis shirt, a style subsequently known as the polo shirt. Attempts have been constantly made by other manufacturers to reproduce the unique collar of this sports shirt, patented as the 'Vestee'. This comprises not the usual two-piece placket but a single piece of knitted fabric that is attached to both sides of the collar, turning at the bottom to produce a flat three-button opening. Although initially worn for tennis, the shirt was produced in several colours. There are five machines unique to Smedley that are currently in use to produce both this classic style and one called Dorset.

The John Smedley company has been a family-owned business for 225 years, utilizing production methods and handcrafted finishing techniques that have been passed down through the generations while also exploiting modern technology. The factory was founded in 1784 by John Smedley and Peter Nightingale near Matlock in Derbyshire, England, 13 years after Richard Arkwright developed the first water-powered spinning mill in 1771 in nearby Cromford. Initially specializing in the production of muslin and spinning cotton, supplying outworkers in nearby cottages with yarn for their hand-frame looms, by the end of the eighteenth century the company had extended its activities to include knitting and hosiery manufacture within the factory system. Upon his death in 1875 the second John Smedley had no heir, thus the business was passed onto a third John, a cousin J T Marsden Smedley, who after his death in 1877 entrusted the company to his son, the fourth John B Marsden Smedley. He remained chairman for 70 years, installing up-to-the-minute knitting machines and forming a limited company in 1893. Production expanded to include underwear and knitted outerwear.

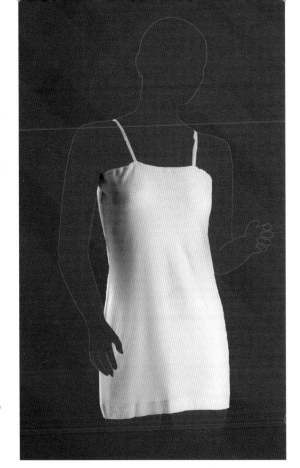

John Smedley is renowned for knitting fully fashioned, fine-gauge products resulting in an ultra-lightweight fine knit, rarely produced by other manufacturers. The company's policy was described in a sales document in 1934:

It is as necessary to spin good yarn in fact as in fable, and the success of the manufacturer rests to a large extent on this knowledge. He must not only know the very source of his material but supervise each process it undergoes from the beginning... The best Australian lamb's wool, silk, cashmere and other fibres, are brought to Lea Mills, where each is treated and blended in the manner best suited to before being spun into yarns. There, they undergo the spinning, the proper doubling and twisting before all is ready for full fashioned knitting. The complete coordination between the departments – each so different, yet each in the same building – results in the achievement of the perfect blend of fabric appropriate to each type of garment. Our outstanding speciality is that the garments are mainly manufactured on the full fashioned frames, of which we believe we have the largest and the most up-to-date in the world.

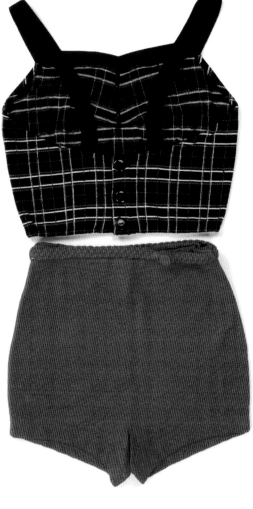

Above Back view of a 1920s two-piece bathing costume by John Smedley. To enhance its functionality, the fabric is robust and relatively inelastic. The check effect is attained by crossing horizontal weft stripes with vertical warp stripes, introduced by 'lace bars' and adding fine warp lines of colour.

The John Smedley company continued to manufacture both men and women's underwear in the 1930s, including the traditional combinations and directoire knickers in cashmere, angora and silk mixtures and the lighter spun silk, and the Milanese and Jaylax lace underwear. Women's petticoats now reflected the shapelier silhouette of the decade, having fully-fashioned bra tops. Not only were the traditional white and pink colours used, checks and stripes appeared on knickers and pants for men. Smedley's were also producing fashion-led knitwear. Matching cardigans and jumpers were more versatile than the simple twinset, the jumper featuring design details such as a collar and short sleeves. Underwear and nightwear began to evolve into leisurewear, with silk 'Nightie-Pyjamas with a matching Boudoir wrap' and fine rayon and wool mixture palazzo trousers with a pintucked waist and matching top of cap sleeves and bow. John Smedley exported to those areas with which they already had a trading relationship from importing silk and cotton: Burma, the Malay states, China, Japan, the Dutch East Indies, Siam, Australia, South Africa and Rhodesia, France, Italy, Belgium, Norway, Sweden, Denmark and Holland.

Types of wool

Wool is the most commonly used yarn for knitted garments. For centuries, sheep have provided mankind with both food and clothing. Wool is durable, flexible and ecologically sound.

The quality of wool that sheep produce varies according to breed and location. Merino sheep, originally a Spanish breed, produce wool that is noted for its whiteness and fineness. Lambswool is wool sheared from a lamb between 11 and 12 months old, the first year clip. Merino comes from the second year clip and is considered the most valuable of wools. Australia produces about 43 per cent of the world's Merino wool. Any wool taken from the sheep in subsequent years is suitable only for blankets and carpets.

Shetland wool is the clip of lambs from the Shetland Islands and North of Scotland, where the colder climate produces a heavier yarn.

United States sheep producers raise four breeds of sheep that produce fine wool and fifteen breeds that produce medium-grade and coarse wools. The medium-grade wool comes from breeds raised primarily for food. Although sheep producers exist in all States (except Hawaii), most sheep operations are in the West.

The production process

Shearing: Sheep are sheared once a year, usually in the spring. The wool is trimmed in one piece, called a fleece.

Scouring: The fleece is washed to remove impurities, such as dirt, grease and dried sweat. Impurities account for between 30 and 70 per cent of the fleece weight. At this point, the wool is considered cleaned wool or scoured wool. The grease that is removed is considered a valuable by-product. Lanolin, in its purified state, is used in creams, soaps, lotions, cosmetics and ointments.

Dyeing: In quality garments, the fleece would be dyed. In inferior-quality garments the colour is added at the yarn stage.

Carding: The wool is combed to straighten the fibres.

Spinning: Once straightened, the fibres can be spun into yarn. The thread produced by a process of spinning is called a single yarn. This is unsuitable for hand-knitting. Two, three or four ends of a single yarn are twisted together to produce two-, three- or four-ply wool.

Fancy yarns

A yarn is any kind of spun thread. Fancy yarns are yarns that differ from the normal construction by the deliberate introduction of irregularities such as knots, loops, curls, slubs, and so on.

Bouclé: Yarns with a twisted core with an effect wrapped around it so it produces the distinctive looped surface.

Chenille yarn: A yarn that has a cut pile consisting of a variety of fibres helically disposed around axial threads which secure it.

Crepe: A highly twisted yarn. Also moss crepe yarn, a two-ply yarn made by doubling a normal twist with a high-twist yarn.

Fair Isle Knits

Golf was the sport of choice for the Duke of Windsor, who later became Edward VIII. When the prince appeared in a Fair Isle sleeveless pullover while playing golf, the indigenous knitwear went from being a local speciality and tourist keepsake to the pages of the fashion magazines.

He later recorded the event in his book, *A Family Album*: 'I suppose the most showy of all my garments was the multi-coloured Fair Isle sweater with its jigsaw pattern, which I wore for the first time while playing myself in as Captain of the Royal & Ancient Golf Club at St Andrews in 1922.'

Originally found on the small Scottish island between Orkney and Shetland, Fair Isle jumpers were initially made to supplement the income from fishing and farming. It was a craft that needed little equipment and a skill that could be passed down the generations and was, at times, practised by men and women alike. The earliest museum samples date from 1850, but the patterned knitwear was first mentioned by Samuel Hibbert as bright caps of 'fantastical colours' worn by the Shetland men in his *A Description of the Shetland Islands* in 1822. Although travellers to the area noted multicoloured gloves and stockings (socks) being worn, there is no evidence of the jumpers being made before 1914.

The attention given to Prince Edward's sartorial choice led to a large increase in production on the island during the 1920s, when Shetland knitters then expanded their work to include hats, gloves and cardigans. The Fair Isle sleeveless jumper (later called a 'tank top') became a vital item in the wardrobe of the male dandies of the era. Initially worn for sporting activities, the patterned sweater was seen on every fashionable undergraduate, worn with 'Oxford bags', the wide-legged trousers that covered the shoes.

The earliest examples of yarn used for Fair Isle knitting were from the island's indigenous sheep and left undyed in their natural colours of white, grey and brown. Later colour was introduced by dyeing the yarn with various lichens. Yellow was produced from onion skins, and expensive madder and indigo were imported to the island to produce red and blue. Although traditional colour schemes were yellow and white motifs on a ground of banded red, indigo and black, the 1920s propensity for beige resulted in the background colours generally being restricted to fawn, grey or 'game-fleck', like the plumage of a partridge.

The typical patterning of the original Fair Isle was made up of horizontal bands of colour, usually less than 15 rows deep. The separation of circular motifs by four diagonal corners produced the so-called OXO designs, the X with a vertical line running through its centre. As time progressed, other motifs were added to the vocabulary of the knitters. Patterns often included symbols that held special meaning: the cross for faith, the anchor for hope and the heart for charity. The simplest method of knitting a coloured pattern is to work together two threads of different colours, stranding the unused yarn behind the working yarn at each stitch. No more than two or three colours can be used, as the

Opposite A portrait of HRH The Prince of Wales from 1925 by John St Helier Lander shows the Duke in his favourite jigsaw-patterned Fair Isle sweater.

Overleaf Men's jumpers showing variations in colour and patterning of the Fair Isle knitting technique from the Fair Isle Knitwear Group, dating from 1920–30.

strands would be too long for practicality. The resulting double thickness of a jumper knitted in this style provided ideal protection against the damp and cold of the northern European weather, being warm and flexible yet durable. Although production burgeoned during the 1920s, pattern books were rarely used until enterprising islanders, Mary Johnstone and her brother, produced graphs of the designs for commercial purposes from 1927.

Traditional Fair Isle sweater construction usually involves knitting the body of the sweater in the round, sewing or otherwise fastening the work securely where the armholes are to go, and then cutting the knit fabric to make the armholes. These cuts are known as 'steeks' in American knitting technology but not in the Shetland Isles, where the Fair Isle technique was developed. This tradition and skill has been handed down from generation to generation. Although the term 'Fair Isle' is used to describe the style of pattern, true Fair Isle pieces are only knitted in the Shetlands. In recent years Fair Isle has inspired designs by Missoni, Ralph Lauren, Alexander McQueen and Burberry, though the yarn used is more likely to be cashmere than Shetland wool.

Below Vacationing socialite Miss Rachel Wallace of Boston, Massachusetts, signifies her leisure status at Hot Springs, Vancouver, by adopting the folk-patterning of a Scandinavian sweater. The look is rendered more urbane by the detachable linen collar and cuffs plus coordinated leather belt and correspondent shoes.

Stitch variations

Cable stitch: Two or more groups of adjacent wales that pass under and over one another to give the effect of a plaited rope.

Intarsia: Weft knitted plain, rib or purl fabrics with designs in two or more colours within the same course. Each area of colour is knitted from a separate length of yarn.

Lace stitch: Openwork effect made by transferring needle loops to an adjacent needle of the same needle bar.

Picot: In knitting, picot edges or hems are produced by making a row of lace eyelets in stocking or plain stitch and then making a fold of fabric with the holes along the folded edge, forming small scallops.

Racked stitch: A sideways deflected stitch that lies across a stitch formed in the same course on the opposite needle bed and has a ric-rac effect.

Raschel lace: Lace fabric produced on a raschel warp-knitting machine.

Space-dyeing: Production of multicolour yarns by applications of various colorants at intervals along a yarn, producing a multicoloured fabric from a single thread.

Terry: Uncut loops in fabric, associated with towelling.

Velour, warp knitted: A two- or three-bar warp knitted fabric in which a pile is produced. The fabric is cropped after raising.

Elsa Schiaparelli

While Chanel designed wearable clothes of an easy elegance, her rival, Elsa Schiaparelli, produced garments that challenged the wearer and combined the avant-garde with high-octane glamour. Born into a family of wealthy intellectuals, the designer was a close friend of the poets, philosophers and artists of the day including Salvador Dalí, Man Ray and Picasso. Her fashion was always concerned with ideas, while Chanel's aesthetic was much more to do with lifestyle. Schiaparelli's first excursion into design had an immediate effect. In the words of her autobiography, *A Shocking Life*, when she introduced her iconic trompe l'oeil bow sweater to Parisian society, 'All the women wanted one, immediately.'

Intrigued by the hand-knitted sweater of a friend, Schiaparelli discovered that its firmer texture was the result of a technique deploying a three-needle stretch-resistant process, which produced a tweed-like effect. This was achieved by carrying the white yarn across the back of the black yarn and catching it behind every third or fourth stitch as it was being knitted. The technique was the work of Armenian immigrants, Arousiag Mikaelian and her brother, who produced knitted goods for the wholesale trade. Although Schiaparelli herself did not know how to knit, saying 'the art of clicking those two little metal needles and making them produce something has always been a mystery to me,' she describes the collaboration with the knitters:

> I drew a large butterfly bow in front, like a scarf around the neck – the primitive drawing of a child of prehistoric times. I said, 'The bow must be white against a black background, and there will be white underneath.' The first sweater was not a success. It came out lopsided and not at all attractive. The second was better. The third I thought sensational.

The fashion editor of the December issue of American *Vogue* magazine agreed, describing the sweater as a 'masterpiece'. The first order, for 40 sweaters with matching skirts, was completed in two weeks. Orders from American sportswear wholesaler W H Davidow Sons followed, and by 1928 the design was so ubiquitous that knitting instructions appeared in the popular American magazine *Ladies' Home Journal* without attributing its source.

Copying was rife – Schiaparelli was not the only victim. Replicas of hand-knitted sweaters by Jean Regny and Lucien Lelong were advertised by New York department store Macy's in *The New York Times*. It was the custom for a single garment to be purchased direct from the designer and then copied for the mass-production market at a greatly reduced price. However, Schiaparelli was resigned: 'the moment that people stop copying you, it means that you are no longer any good and that you have ceased to be news.'

In 1928 Schiaparelli moved to 4 rue de la Paix, and erected a black-and-white sign Pour le Sport on the front door. From here the designer produced a

Opposite Parisian couturier Elsa Schiaparelli (1890–1973) photographed in the 1950s by Sylvia Salmi.

Right The celebrated, best-selling sweater designed by Elsa Schiaparelli with a trompe l'oeil graphic bow at the neck. The bow is created using a classic Fair Isle structure, where any yarn not required in the face side is carried across the reverse and caught into the back of the stitches to avoid long 'floats'. This technique forms a uniformly less elastic knit.

Opposite A grey hand-knit sweater-coat with black bone buttons designed by Schiaparelli is modelled by Muriel Finley and photographed by Edward Steichen in 1928. The structured tailoring of the collar and patch pockets contrasts with the soft, loose-knitted texture of the jacket, which is accessorized with a cloche hat designed by Rose Valois.

collection of hand-knitted sweaters, coats, skirts, bathing suits and crocheted berets. Some sweaters utilized the new elastic woollen fabric, kasha, which clung provocatively to the body. The trompe l'oeil effects now included faux scarves, neckties and belts, and more avant-garde subject matter. She writes:

One was tattooed like a sailor's chest with pierced hearts and snakes. There was a skeleton sweater that shocked the bourgeois but hit the newspapers, which then took little notice of fashion. White lines on the sweater followed the design of the ribs so that women wearing it gave the appearance of being seen through an X-ray… and fish wriggling on the stomach for a bathing suit.

The designer's innovations were not restricted to surface decoration. Her first patent was for a backless bathing suit that incorporated a brassière with straps that crossed low on the back and fastened in the front at the waist, made in a thick herringbone-striped knit. Schiaparelli had enormous international commercial success with a tiny knitted cap like a tube; the 'mad-cap' could be pulled into a variety of shapes and, like the bow-front sweater, was copied in the thousands.

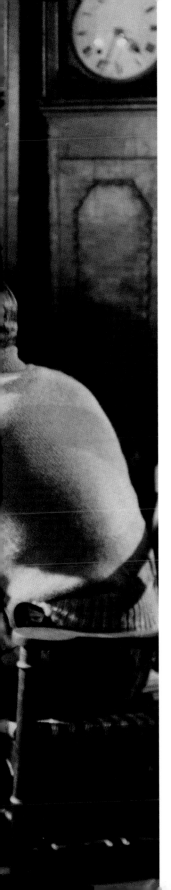

Fabric types

Cloqué fabric or blister fabric: A rib-based fabric with a relief pattern which may be a different colour from the ground.

Double jersey (weft knitting): A generic name applied to a range of knitted fabrics made on a rib or interlock basis, the construction of which is often designed to reduce the 'stretchability' of the structure.

Felted fabric: A fabric where the fibres have been matted together during the processing or in use.

Fleece fabric: A plain weft-knitted fabric with a ground yarn and in which a yarn of low twist, secured by a binder, appears on the back of the fabric and may be brushed or raised.

Laid-in fabric, weft-knitted: A fabric containing non-knitted yarns which are held in position by the knitted structure.

Plain fabric: A fabric in which all the component knitted loops are of the same sort and meshed in the same manner.

Plated fabric: A fabric knitted from two yarns of different properties, producing a reversible design.

Purl fabric: A fabric in which both back and face loops are in some or all of the wales, or rows.

Rib fabric: A weft-knitted fabric in which both back and face loops of the same type occur along the course, forming a strong elasticized edge to a garment hem or cuff.

Single jersey: A generic name applied to knitted fabrics made on a plain knitted base. In hand-knitting it is then called stocking stitch.

Left Couples enjoy a late-afternoon après-ski dance in Switzerland, photographed by George Hoyningen-Huene in 1929. The skiing suit and belted sweater (left) were designed by Schiaparelli, while French couturier Jane Regny created the triangle-patterned belted sweater and knit cap (centre) and military-inspired sweater with large buttons, belt and trim in contrasting colour (right).

The Modernist Shoe

Modernism changed the look of the shoe in the 1920s, as Cubist aesthetics, Bauhaus austerity and American streamlining entered the vocabulary of the designer in the form of Art Deco. This style reached its apotheosis at the *Exposition des Arts Décoratifs*, held in Paris in 1924, where the exhibits revealed the hallmarks of this innovative style: a combination of clear lines and geometric shapes rendered out of the most deluxe of materials.

Shoes followed suit and as their lines became increasingly simple, so the materials used to make the uppers became more exotic. Colours were bold and bright and surface decoration graphic – Chinese, Cubist or Egyptian-inspired after the discovery of Tutankhamen's tomb in 1922. Rows of buttons and intricate laces, so popular at the beginning of the century, were rejected in favour of styles that had more visual clarity, such as single side buttons and T-bar shapes. Cuban heels took over from the hourglass Louis heel and, when affixed to evening shoes, were extravagantly decorated with rhinestones, mock tortoiseshell or cloisonné enamel.

The uncluttered silhouettes of Paul Poiret influenced a new generation of couturiers including Coco Chanel and Madeleine Vionnet, who presented a sportif silhouette that reflected the prevailing zeitgeist of youth and modernity and revealed, as Chanel described, 'the death of luxury'. Luxury was still there, however, albeit in a more understated form of 'deluxe poverty'. Simple cloche hats were worn over short, chic bobbed haircuts, and womanly hips and breasts were out of fashion. In their place came a more elegantly androgynous, tubular look, with simple skirts hovering around the knee, which gave focus to the entire shoe rather than just the toe as in previous years.

The painted faces and short hemlines of the flappers presented a more overt sexuality when sashaying down the city streets and caused alarm among more traditional members of the public, who suspected, quite rightly, that fashionable femininity was in transition. Women claimed the right to roam and by so doing were breaking societal and sometimes sartorial codes. By appearing on their own, without male chaperones on the city streets, wearing obvious make-up and brazenly smoking Russian cigarettes from ivory holders, they were playing with the codes of femininity by aping the modes and manners of the vamp.

Dance Shoes and Decoration

Edwardian society had retained vestiges of the aristocratic but the 1920s were different; class structure was beginning to break down and many more members of the community shared an increased prosperity and better living conditions. More money was being spent on fashion and more money was being spent on fun. The two came together in the dance revolution that had begun with the Argentinean tango and was expressed in an even wilder way with the dance innovations of the 1920s.

The rise of ragtime and jazz – syncopated, rhythmic musical forms originating from black America – brought about a new freedom in dancing and created energetic styles such as the Bunny Hug, where couples pressed their bodies tightly together, and the fast-paced Turkey Trot, a spirited reaction against the inhibited and formal movements of the traditional waltz. In 1919, one vicar was even moved to protest, 'If these up-to-date dances, described as the 'latest craze' are within a hundred miles of all I hear about them, I should say that the morals of a pig-sty would be respectable in comparison.'

The Charleston was no better, introduced to the American public as part of the Ziegfeld Follies show *Runnin' Wild* in 1923, and reaching Europe by 1925. Its celebrated side-kicks and exaggerated play with the knees required a much sturdier shoe for women to participate with any degree of athleticism. Shoes became more securely fitted to the feet, with low Cuban heels and closed toes, and beaded decoration and metallic threadwork that glittered in the lights of a smoky speakeasy. When matched with a beaded and fringed dance dress, women shimmered spectacularly in contrast to their black-suited partners. If more glitz was needed, an array of shoe clips were available in the form of birds, Egyptian scarabs and butterflies, which could be added to little black day shoes to create instant party feet. Cubist patterns, hand-painted Chinoiserie and daring colour combinations entered the market – a cacophony of gold and red kidskin, sky-blue and emerald-green satin, or more subtle black velvet with steel beadwork. More prosaically, improved manufacturing processes meant that significantly cheaper shoes were available, so many were chosen simply because of their looks rather than their more practical function.

Opposite The latest white fur fashion and cloche hat is teamed with burnished satin evening shoes with bar straps, circa 1926. The new flapper style emphasized a long leg and shapely ankle, rather than the Edwardian hourglass silhouette.

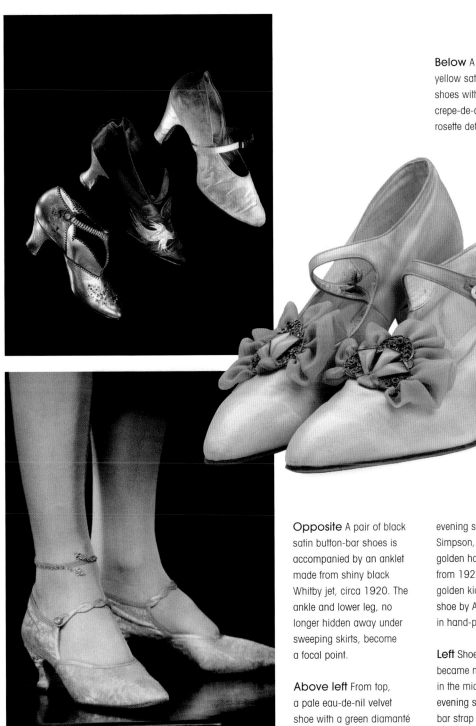

Below A pair of buttercup yellow satin pearl-button bar shoes with a darker toned crepe-de-chine and turquoise rosette detail, circa 1920–25.

Opposite A pair of black satin button-bar shoes is accompanied by an anklet made from shiny black Whitby jet, circa 1920. The ankle and lower leg, no longer hidden away under sweeping skirts, become a focal point.

Above left From top, a pale eau-de-nil velvet shoe with a green diamanté fastening from Edward Rayne, 1928; a brown satin evening shoe by Stead and Simpson, decorated with a golden hand-painted phoenix from 1922; and a 1925 golden kidskin T-bar dancing shoe by A Rambaldi, covered in hand-painted flowers.

Left Shoes and stockings became more decorative in the mid-1920s. Here, evening shoes with a crossed bar strap are teamed with stockings embellished with a faux gem ankle bracelet.

Right A bobbed flapper shows off a selection of shoe jewellery, circa 1928. Clips were an easy and cheap way to completely change the look of a simple evening shoe and could be used to complement any shade of evening gown.

Below A brocade shoe of 1925 has the additional glamour of a pearl-studded silver buckle.

Opposite A minimalist yet deluxe Art Deco interior, all simple lines and glamorous fashion. A model sports a cocktail dress with velvet skirt and elegant high-heeled evening pumps with square rhinestone-studded shoe clips, circa 1928.

Decorative elements

- Shoe clips, especially in insect and butterfly shapes, that could be added to shoes for an instant party feel
- Geometric Cubist patterns
- Hand-painted chinoiserie details
- Daring colour combinations such as silver and tango orange
- Metallic threadwork and beadwork
- Egyptian and Native American motifs
- Heels made of Bakelite, Wedgwood and Jasperware, and then decorated with rhinestones and beading

A key change in the 1920s was the disappearance of the boot, so beloved of the Edwardian woman. The newly shortened skirt created an unsightly gap between the top of the boot and the hem of the skirt, a gap that yawned wider and wider as the decade progressed. Eventually, boots were ditched in favour of short-toed bar shoes with high wooden heels and sheer stockings, which made the legs (and an artfully rouged pair of knees) look enticingly erotic. Rubber galoshes or overshoes were worn during inclement weather, which removed the necessity for boots, another reason for their demise. Many young women refused to fasten the buckles that secured the galosh about the ankle, leaving it flapping rather wetly against the calf. This relaxed informal look, some believe, gave rise to the word 'flapper' to describe the new, seemingly strident young woman of the 1920s.

Such an abrupt change in footwear etiquette shocked the older generation, who had very strict ideas about what should be worn, where, and when. As early as 1916, the *Shoe and Leather Lexicon*, an American trade magazine, wrote that 'Women have shown a tendency in late years to wear on the street shoes suitable only for indoor use… desiring to drag boudoir suggestiveness through the streets.' In the 1920s, the standards of usage began to seriously slip quite simply because with so many styles to choose from, young women were determined to wear whatever they pleased. A few rules still applied, however, although they were less rigorously implemented than in the previous decade:

Day shoes covered more of the foot than those designated as eveningwear, which had lower-cut vamps (upper parts).

Stacked leather heels were for practical daywear; the dressier Louis heel was for night. Evening shoes had higher and more thinly tapered heels.

Toe caps signified a day shoe; plain toes were for the evening.

Sport shoes had brogueing or perforation along the seams, following the rules of traditional male sports footwear.

Suede and leather in brown or black were supposed to be for daywear, and fabric for night only, although many women ignored this distinction.

Opposite A winter outfit of fur-trimmed coat and boots with spats, circa 1925. Boots had become items of functional footwear rather than being worn for everyday as in the preceeding decades. They only appeared when needed in inclement weather.

Below The Hollywood actress Bessie Love, circa 1928, is ready for the rain. Galoshes were worn unfastened to give a more casual girl-about-town look. Their untidy appearance gave rise to the epithet 'flapper'.

Left A line of chorus girls from *The Girl from Cooks* show, 1927, display T-bar, split-bar and strappy cut-out dancing shoes.

Above Ladies' solo Charleston champion Miss Hardie, who danced for a record seven hours in 1925, wears low sturdy heels and a bar strap to keep her shoes secure during her energetic dance routine.

The Mary Jane and Signature Shoes

The Mary Jane was a broad, closed-toed shoe with a flat single strap that fastened across the instep, with a button to the side and a low heel. It has a long history as a child's shoe and can be seen in Tudor paintings of the sixteenth century. This shoe had important symbolic associations because it traditionally signalled a child's transition from baby to toddler, as it was worn when a child took his or her first tentative steps. The shoe thus symbolized a significant rite of passsage

By the early twentieth century, this eminently practical style of footwear was yet to be given a gender and remained a unisex children's shoe. It was worn by such resonant childhood fictional characters as Alice from *Alice in Wonderland*, and Christopher Robin in the well-known illustrations by EH Shepherd for AA Milne's *Winnie the Pooh*. However, events conspired to make this shoe feminine, an item that was deemed fit only for a woman's wardrobe, and that is where it remains to this day.

EVENING SHOES OF BROCHÉ AND BROCADE

In 1902, a cartoon strip called 'Buster Brown' appeared in the *New York Herald* newspaper, created by graphic artist Richard F Outcault and featuring a group of mischievous children, which included the eponymous Buster Brown, his dog, Tige, and his sister, Mary Jane. The popularity of the cartoon was that in 1904, Outcault visited the St Louis World's Fair with the express intention of cashing in on his creations. He allowed 200 manufacturers licences to use his characters as brand names, one of which was the Brown Shoe Company, which had been set up with the life savings of one George Warren Brown in 1878.

Buster Brown became the brand that built the shoe empire that the Brown Shoe Company is today, with its annual turnover of over $2 billion. The company's success is in part due to this licensing deal, which was used to create a pioneering marketing campaign. From 1904 onwards, a roadshow travelled across America visiting department stores and shoe shops, featuring actors dressed as characters from the cartoon strip. Thousands of clamouring kids persuaded their mothers to buy into the brand name, in an early example of cartoon merchandizing that pre-dated Walt Disney.

Mary Jane, Buster Brown's sister, was immortalized when her name was applied to single-strap children's shoes in 1909, and the shoes were gradually transformed into items of female dress, eventually disappearing from the male wardrobe. Their sugary sweet feminine associations were also fused on celluloid when adopted by Shirley Temple. She first tap danced her way across the silver screen in the shoes in 1922's *Baby Burlesk*, and they continued to be her only

Above Evening shoes of 1925. Both day and evening styles became increasingly decorative and combined multicoloured leather with fabrics such as brocade, satin and silk. Heels were higher and more tapered.

Opposite A Liberty's of London outfit from 1928, worn with a simple leather bar shoe, a 1920s fashion favourite. The Mary Jane was a version of this standard item of footwear with a rounder toe and shorter heel.

form of footwear during her reign as the world's most popular child star. With her carefully coiffed ringlets, fixed grin and party dresses puffed out with starched petticoats, Shirley Temple gave Mary Jane shoes an image of such exaggerated girliness that it was only really shaken off by the post-Modernist play of ravaged rock star Courtney Love and her ironic Mary Jane wearing in the 1990s.

When flappers adopted the Mary Jane shoe in the 1920s, they were deliberately choosing a shoe style that evoked youthfulness – the aesthetic that was the prime force behind fashionable trends, in particular the slim, streamlined, almost schoolgirl silhouette with flattened breasts and skirts that skimmed the hips. Fashions of the 1920s deliberately rejected any hint of the matron, and the Mary Jane shoe, the most childish of shoe shapes, was a perfect foil for this fashion.

Over the decade, though, Mary Janes subtly changed and towards the end of the 1920s, their heels became higher and more tapered, their plain cloth or leather uppers more deluxe, and the look of innocence subverted with the use of sensuous satins, heavy brocades and hand-painted silks. The little girl appeared to be growing up.

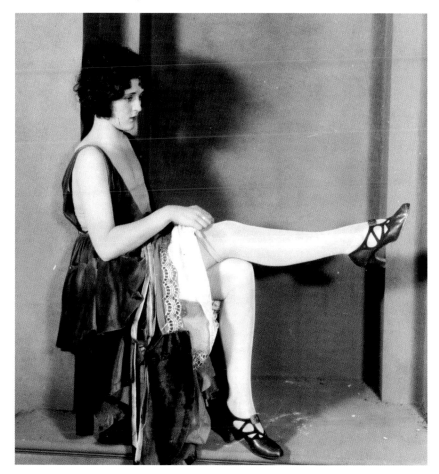

Opposite A fashion model wears a sleeveless loose-fitting dress with a monochromatic striped and fringed skirt, double-strap Mary Jane shoes and a headband, circa 1925.

Left American actress Eleanor Boardman is seen here wearing late 1920s cutaway shoes with front-fastening clasps.

The strapped shoe

The most innovative design detail in 1920s shoes was the use of elaborate strapwork. This was a fashion element that started out with shoes that incorporated one, or occasionally two, horizontal straps with contrasting coloured stitching fastened with a simple button at the side. By 1922, the T-strap was introduced, a strap that ran vertically down the front of the shoe with another strap across to form a 'T' shape, again fastened at the side with a button. The new T-strap was often delineated in contrasting colours so as to stand out against the rest of the shoe. It was an instant success, as it streamlined a woman's foot while saucily exposing it, evoking a frisson of fashionable bondage while simultaneously creating an elegantly Modernist shape that was the height of fashion.

The use of strapwork in shoe design continued, becoming almost fetishist in its application by the middle of the decade. In 1923, for instance, the back of the shoe was extended up the ankle to form an ankle strap that was then fixed to a T-bar in the front. Faux strapwork was also popular, taking the form of intricate leather cut-outs that covered the sides and front of shoes in a finely wrought filigree of leather, which was edged in gold, silver and contrasting coloured skin on the most expensive shoes. Fixed buckles began to take over from buttons as fastening devices and continued to be popular into the 1930s, either in simple steel or more elaborate Art Deco designs studded with sparkling marcasite.

This page and opposite
Illustrations of high-heeled court shoes with elongated toes, shown in the *Gazette du Bon Ton* magazine of 1924. Clockwise, from opposite top left: a multiple loop shoe; a double-loop shoe; a style with a strap secured with a leaf-shaped bar; and a T-bar.

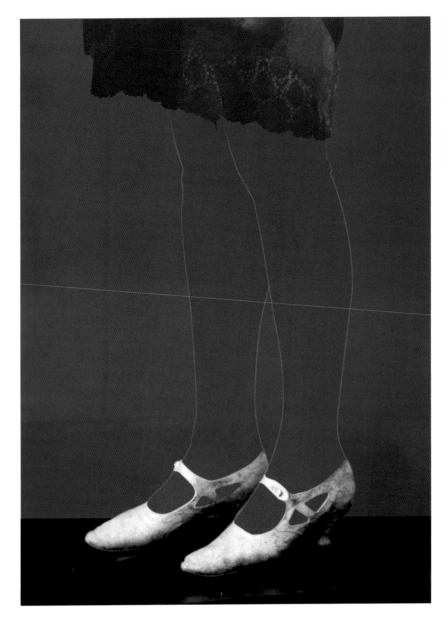

Left These decoratively cutaway bar shoes with Louis heels are from the early 1920s.

Opposite Silver metallic T-bar shoes with a Louis heel worn with patterned stockings and a metal garter, fresh from 1920s Paris.

The Russian boot

The solid leg boot with no fastenings in an easy pull-on, pull-off style had first appeared for women in 1915, but this experimental style failed to catch on possibly because skirts were just too long for the boot to be practical. It was re-introduced with more success as the Russian boot in 1921.

The 1920s Russian boot was knee high, wide topped and flat, based on the traditional Russian *valenki*, a boot that had been developed to cope with the severe winters of Siberia. The *valenki* was a rustic boot, similar in shape to a Wellington or an Australian Ugg boot today, and was made out of thick felt with no seams. Its function, practicality and ease of removal had made it a key part of the Russian soldier's winter kit by the nineteenth century.

Young flappers adopted the silhouette of the valenki when it was re-created as a fashion rather than folk item, rendered in leather and given a low Louis or Cuban heel in 1921. In 1927, the style was endorsed by Hollywood star Gloria Swanson when she advertised a pair of Russian boots for Sears, Roebuck and Company – quite a brave step to take, as by then Russian boots had developed a reputation as the chosen form of footwear for girls who flirted with the underworld.

In 1922, a young woman in Chicago had been photographed in a speakeasy mischievously concealing a flask of illegal liquor down the side of one boot – a perfect illustration of the practice of 'bootlegging', a term that dates back to the nineteenth century. Bootleggers were those who hid whiskey in their boot tops when going to trade with Native Americans, and it became a byword for criminals involved in the illegal transportation of alcohol across state lines. By 1920, bootlegging had become a part of general vocabulary when the National Prohibition Act was passed banning the export, import, transportation, selling and manufacture of alcohol in an attempt to reduce crime and promote healthy and moral lifestyles.

Drinking went underground as illegal speakeasies and saloon bars flourished in most major American cities and every town had its own illegal still, making cheap moonshine for those who wished to imbibe. The Russian boot evoked the image of a woman who walked on the wild side, who was prepared to risk her reputation in order to have a good time – and it was a much sexier alternative to rubber galoshes. By 1930, however, the style had peaked and died, destined to lie dormant until the 1960s.

Above Russian boots were wide at the top – ideal for hiding hip flasks in the Prohibition era and said to be the origin of the word 'bootlegging'. This photograph dates from 1922.

The Oxford

Sometimes referred to as the Balmoral in the United Kingdom, the Oxford is a classic piece of male footwear design that laces up in the front, usually through three pairs of eyelets; it has a tongue to protect the foot from the pressure of the fastenings, curved side seams and a low-stacked leather heel. By the early twentieth century, this practical and comfortable style had been adopted by women and it became the most favoured style of street shoe in the 1920s, when a 5-cm (2-inch) heel was added. The heels became higher and more finely tapered by the middle years of the decade, as the shoe moved from being a staple of the male wardrobe into a female form of fashion.

There were many nuances in women's Oxford shoe design, all appropriated from traditional male footwear styles. The laces were enclosed, wingtips (so-called because the shape resembled the spread wings of a bird) or brogueing detail were sometimes added as perforated panels of decoration along the sides and across the toes, and a small piece of leather was often stitched over the toe to create a toe cap. Saddle Oxfords had a saddle-shaped section sewn onto the upper quarter of the vamp that was of a contrasting colour to the rest of the shoe.

Sports Oxfords or 'spectator' shoes, so-called because they were supposed to be worn by spectators standing on the sidelines of sporting events, had heels and saddles of a different colour to the rest of the shoe. As many spectator shoes had vamps of white canvas, the toes and heels were made of leather to protect the parts of the shoe that were liable to scuff. Popular colour combinations were black and white patent or brown and tan leather, and the more fashion-forward girl about town wore a mix of shiny black patent and brightly coloured reptile skin.

Between 1925 and 1927, the fashion for cut-outs infiltrated the Oxford, appearing next to the eyelets and banishing the tongue, and the toes became so elongated that it was difficult to tell whether the style was actually an Oxford or not. This rather mongrel shoe type was given the catch-all term of semi-Oxford.

Below left and right
An elegant 1926 high-heeled two-toned Oxford shoe with brogueing perforations and wingtip detail by André Perugia.

Mistinguett

Legs, feet and shoes were more overtly displayed in this decade than ever before and the display of a neat pair of pins in beige artificial silk stockings presented what appeared to be a naked leg, creating a new area of erotic interest for men. The most beautiful pair were the property of French showgirl Mistinguett, who was the toast of Paris in the 1920s and was rumoured to have insured her legs for a million dollars. They were displayed to stunning effect during her long-running residency at the Folies Bergère. The climax of the show had Mistinguett – resplendent in an ostrich-feather headdress that weighed 7 kilograms (15 pounds) and a stage outfit with a 25-metre (82-foot) long train – descend a steep staircase in very high heels. Little did the rapt audience know that her eyes were tightly shut to aid concentration and overcome vertigo, because a pair of fake eyes were painted on her closed eyelids in stage make-up.

When off stage, Mistinguett still showed her legs to their best advantage and highlighted them with exaggeratedly high heels, created by the celebrated shoe designer André Perugia. For Mistinguett he fashioned a pair of extravagantly fetishist mules with green suede heels, gold speckled suede vamps in a trompe l'oeil speckled leather effect, to mimic snakeskin, and a vampish ocelot edging – perhaps the most overtly erotic pairs of shoes ever made.

Opposite An illustrative poster of 1913 depicts a seductive Mistinguett wearing elaborately decorative fantasy footwear.

Below The infamous French showgirl and music-hall star Mistinguett with her vast collection of high-heeled shoes. She shows off her celebrated legs.

MISTINGUETT

G.K. Benda

Andr√© Perugia (1893–1977)

Known for his experimentation with new materials, shapes and textures, André Perugia's shoe designs dominated high-end footwear fashion in the 1920s and remain some of the most innovative and experimental footwear ever created for women. Perugia's most successful work was for Saks Fifth Avenue, who distributed his ready-to-wear Padova brand, the American company I Miller, with whom he had a 50-year association, and Charles Jourdan, for whom he was a technical advisor from 1962 to 1966. Like Pietro Yanturni, Perugia, the son of a cobbler, had a background far removed from the elite world of haute couture, although that is where he eventually made his mark, designing shoes for Jacques Fath, Edward Molyneux and the House of Schiaparelli in the 1930s.

Born in Tuscany, Perugia worked as an apprentice in his father's workshop, which was set up when the family moved to Nice in the early 1900s, and by the age of 16, he had taken over the family business. Nice was a popular seaside location where the rich of Paris gathered to spend languid summers sequestered in the hotels that lined the city's fashionable promenade and to gamble away fortunes in its many casinos. Perugia realized that here was a perfect audience for his wares and persuaded one of the top hotels, the Negresco, to devote a window to his shoe designs.

Not only did he draw the attention of the female patrons, but the window display also caught the eye of Paul Poiret in 1914, who from that moment on took the young Perugia under his wing, inviting him to present his shoes in Poiret's atelier in Paris and to meet a wealthier, more fashion-fixated clientele. Perugia's shoes were also used to accessorize several of the couturier's fashion shows that were being held in Nice during the summer season. However, this potentially lucrative breakthrough in Perugia's career was cut short by the First World War and he was requisitioned to work in an aircraft factory. This seemingly unfortunate turn of events was in fact to have an enormously beneficial impact on his aesthetic. Surrounded by the machinery of the military, Perugia was introduced to engineering techniques that were to transform his ideas about shoe design and lead to the development of a series of prototype aerodynamic heels in steel alloy, which anticipated the stiletto heel of the 1950s. For him, shoe design was about precision; as he put it, 'a pair of shoes must be perfect like an equation, and adjusted to the millimetre like a motor piece.'

André Perugia began to seriously make his name in the 1920s, after opening his own shop on the rue du Faubourg Saint-Honoré in 1921, working with Hollywood film stars Pola Negri and Gloria Swanson, for whom his black lace heels became something of a trademark, and the stage star Josephine Baker, for whom he designed quilted kidskin sandals. He also continued his relationship with Paul Poiret, creating the Arlequinade and Folie shoes, named after two of the House of Poiret's most

Opposite Footwear legend André Perugia in his shoe factory, circa 1951, among a multitude of handmade wooden lasts. For an average shoe style a total of 600 patterns, one for every vamp and quarter, was made to give a full range of lengths and widths. His first boutique opened in 1921.

Below A black-and-beige leather shoe with woven strap, 1924, by Perugia.

popular fragrances. In 1924, in homage to the couturier's patronage, Perugia created Le Bal, a whimsical pair of shoes that celebrated Poiret's renowned love of parties. Each shoe was heavily over-embroidered with a pattern of densely placed seed beads that showed, in vignette form, on one shoe a portrait of Poiret and on the other his wife and muse, Denise – and they caused a fashionable furore when she entered a crowded ballroom.

Every season, Perugia made sure he hit the headlines with some flamboyant experimental design, but these tended to be one-offs. The rest of his time was spent producing chic, wearable shoes that followed the prevailing silhouette, albeit more exquisitely made than most. Thus, his 1920s designs followed the fashion for T-bars and straps with fantastic finishes, such as burnished bronze and gold metal with Art Deco motifs moulded in relief on tapering heels, and intricate Cubist patterns cut out of leather inlay. He became known for using the most remarkable diversity of exotic materials: glossy black horsehair, antelope and alligator, even Peruvian llama. His forte was combining materials such as champagne-coloured satin and metallic brocade or gold leather with velvet dyed exactly the same shade, so as to give a tactile as well as a visual appeal to the shoe. Fastenings were given the same detailed attention: buckles were exquisitely carved and enamelled and buttons took on the shape of diminutive gilded rosebuds.

What differentiated Perugia from earlier footwear designers such as Yanturni or Pinet was that, as a result of his engineering background, he was the first to really understand the ergonomics of shoe design. Like those before him, he always took an impression of the client's foot in plaster of Paris and made detailed measurements, but for him the most fascinating part of shoe design was working out the relationship between the shoe and the heel and how weight was distributed through the body and onto the feet. Suitability, function and the relationship of the shape of the shoe to the correct balance of the heel were, for him, more important than any fashionable design. To this end, he literally took the shoe apart and re-assembled it, achieving designs by the 1950s that totally transformed the look of women's shoes.

Throughout his career, Perugia kept developing totally new methods of manufacture and construction, applying for over 40 patents for his innovative designs such as the corkscrew heel of 1952. Shoes became sculpture in his magical hands; the 'Ode to Industry' shoe of 1950, for instance, was more of an art object than a practical consideration for women, a shoe that paid homage to the new post-war machine age with its iconic heel of twisted steel.

Opposite An illustration of exquisite shoe styles by Perugia: on the left, red-and-gold shoes are worn with a white spaghetti-strapped dress; on the right, purple-and-pink T-bar shoes complement a low-cut tubular dress with pleated side vents. From the *Gazette du Bon Ton*, 1924.

Below left and right
A cutaway double-buttoned black leather shoe, circa 1923, and a satin square-toed mule with cord detail, circa 1925, both by Perugia.

The Bottiers of Paris

By the end of the 1920s, due to the devalued franc, Paris was host to thousands of overseas customers ready to spend their money on fashion. They were drawn to a city that had a number of exclusive bottiers (shoemakers) whose names have all but disappeared today, save for an artfully inscribed name inside a vintage shoe. A Gillet, the Armenian émigré Sarkis del Balian, and Julienne, one of the few female footwear designers of this period, produced outstanding shoes, as did Alfred Argence and Charles Hellstern.

Hellstern was name-checked in the novels of both Nancy Mitford and F Scott Fitzgerald and if a flapper had money to burn, this particular shoe emporium was where she would go to salivate over their silver kid slippers and blood-red suede bar shoes. The firm had been founded in 1870 by Louis Hellstern but underwent a dramatic transformation when the reins were taken up by his sons Maurice, Charles and Henri Hellstern in 1920. Under their directorship, designs became extravagant, dramatic and occasionally luridly extreme. Hellstern's silhouettes were standard 1920s fare but the use of colour and decoration was sublime. Bar shoes could be of the deepest navy-blue velvet, fringed with steel and sparkling with beadwork. Heels could be celluloid or covered with a searing apple-green suede to contrast with bright gold leather uppers. Buttons were rhinestone-studded, and buckles were bedecked with pearls or took the form of huge velvet rosettes. And mistresses caused consternation when staggering around the boudoir in a pair of their 'specialist' black-leather fetish boots with 25-cm (10-inch) heels and a thick platform sole emblazoned with rhinestones.

Opposite Hellstern's trademark deluxe satin pumps with an enamel-and-rhinestone Art Deco buckle and Louis heels. The high-cut vamp encloses the foot.

Below A pair of soft flesh-pink slippers by Hellstern, circa 1910. Hellstern's 1920s shoe shapes were typical of the period but their colour and decoration were exemplary.

HELLSTERN & SONS,
c. 1905

Art Deco Handbags

The 1920s were all about movement, from the flying fringes of the Charleston dress to the streamlined silhouettes of the newly introduced automobiles. Symbols of the new modernity, they came to define the age and signified a break from the past.

Handbags reflected this desire for the new and the modern. The drawstring bag, drooping from a languid wrist, was finally out of style, and the emergence of the clutch propelled the handbag towards the future. Made of Bakelite and Perspex, in the clashing colours and vibrant patterns of the Art Deco movement and the decade's obsession with all things Egyptian, the clutch represented the aesthetic preoccupations of the age.

Aspects of modernism had existed since 1914, in Cubism, Expressionism, Futurism, and abstraction in painting, but it was not until after the war that modernism made its mark on everyday life, from Marcel Breuer's tubular chair, designed in 1925, to the architecture of the Bauhaus, founded in 1919. The post-war world had seen a seismic shift away from the discredited attitudes, hierarchies and prejudices of the prewar world. Manifestos of cultural revolution appeared; the arts influenced fashion and the avant-garde became mainstream. With the advent of modernism, the twentieth century was about to really begin.

Just as stuffy, heavily decorated Victorian interiors and restrictive corsets were rejected, so, too, was the impractical reticule with its dainty flounces and drawstring opening. This was the era when bags became a vital fashion accessory to a total look, rather than merely a useful adjunct. The new bags were streamlined exercises in restraint when decoration was perceived as 'feminine' and trivial, an attitude influenced by the writings of the Austrian architect Adolf Loos. 'Freedom from ornament is a sign of spiritual strength,' he wrote in his defining essay 'Ornament and Crime' in 1908, and he anticipated that with female economic independence, 'velvet and silk, flowers and ribbons, feathers and paint will fail to have their effect.' Certainly, there was an element of androgyny about the rangy, elongated silhouette of a new phenomenon, the 1920s flapper girl.

FLAPPER STYLE

In her short skirts and skimpy tubular dresses with only a flimsy combination of camisole and knickers, known as camiknickers, replacing the whalebone corsets, her breasts flattened and concealed, the flapper represented freedom from all the constraints of the previous century. No lady's maid was required to dress hair that was newly shingled or cropped into an Eton bob. The close-fitting cloche hat replaced towering confections of tulle and flowers, and no reticule dangled from her wrist; rather, a clutch bag was securely tucked between her upper arm and body, or carried in the hand to be opened with a decisive snap as she reached for her lipstick or powder.

The clean, pared-down silhouette of the body was also reflected in the simplicity of the face; the plucked, high-arched eyebrows, almond-shaped eyes, the small rosebud mouth and the flat, head-hugging shingle bob all reflected the influence of the Romanian sculptor Brancusi, whose works included 'Sleeping Muse'. This visage appeared repeatedly on the cover of *Vogue* throughout the decade.

This new generation of 'bright young things' was perceived as decadent and hedonistic, pursuing pleasure with a single-mindedness that went hand in hand with social emancipation. The flapper embodied the spirit of the Jazz Age and moved to the syncopated, rhythmic dance music that originated in black America and was yet another symbol of modernity. When hemlines are raised, the waistline changes; in 1925 it dropped to below the hips. This streamlined style gave the flapper the freedom of movement to embrace her partner for the Turkey Trot or to enjoy the uninhibited Charleston. As the flapper frolicked energetically around the dance floor, her bag had to fulfil certain requirements. It needed a secure clasp, and to be lightweight and small, so it could be grasped securely. For this reason, the tango purse was sometimes fitted with finger rings or lengths of cord that could be wrapped around the wrist. The wit and poet Dorothy Parker, commenting on the new generation's provocative attitudes, wrote in her poem 'The Flapper':

The playful flapper here we see,
The fairest of the fair.
She's not what Grandma used to be,—
You might say, au contraire.
Her girlish ways may make a stir,
Her manners cause a scene,
But there is no more harm in her
Than in a submarine.

Above During the 1920s hemlines reached unprecedented heights, heels got higher and bags got smaller. Laura La Plante, the blonde leading lady of Universal Studios, is standing with her sister, Violet, in a photograph taken in 1928; the bag takes centre stage.

Opposite The neat cloche hat, a popular style of the 1920s, frames a face of immaculate maquillage, reflected in the vanity mirror attached to a hard-framed handbag from 1924.

Vanity cases

The use of cosmetics was perceived as dangerously provocative; 'decent' women wore no make-up, and even dabbing the nose with a French device called a *poudre-papier* was done surreptitiously by Edwardian matrons. In contrast, the flapper brazenly outlined her lips in public and rouged even her earlobes. This daily maquillage required constant refreshment, and handbags took over the role of vanity cases to transport powder, rouge, lipstick and perfume. The shape of the vanity case was attributed to the Japanese *inro*, a small box with compartments for medicinal herbs and perfumed water. Exclusive vanity cases were made by jewellers such as Cartier and Van Cleef & Arpels in silver or gold, enamel, mother of pearl, jade and lapis lazuli. Cheaper versions were made from coloured plastic and decorated with glass stones. Miniature vanity cases often had mini lipstick containers that swung on a length of tassel or were fixed to a Bakelite bangle worn on the lower arm.

The mesh bag manufacturers Whiting & Davis produced vanity or 'function' bags of a dazzling complexity, including the amphora-shaped Delysia, in which the powder puff, rouge puff and mirror were carried in the central hinged section, while the mesh pockets and top and bottom of the bag provided storage. A centre-mounted top strap and an elaborate hanging tassel completed the design, which at that time retailed at $500.

A further novelty was added to the vanity case when the British company Dunhill produced the Lytup bag, which lit up when it was opened. According to *Tatler* magazine in May 1922, it was 'invaluable in a taxi, or wherever the lights were dim'.

Opposite Founded in 1781 as a silk-printing business, Asprey moved to their current premises in New Bond Street, London, in 1847. An early speciality was dressing cases, creating portable designs suitable for the new style of travel. This advertisement for new wares, such as the Mulberry crocodile pochette and a flat-based handbag, appeared in *Tatler* magazine in 1926.

Below Different-sized vanity cases complement the two evening dresses by Maison Gerda, circa 1925.

ASPREY
BOND STREET,
LONDON.

Bronze and Gilt Metal
Cartridge Placefinder.
1 . 10 . 0

Combined Vanity and Cigarette
Case, with Silver-gilt and
Glass Fittings.
7 . 17 . 6

Race
Companion,
Silver-gilt mounts.
Crocodile, 7 . 12 . 6
Pigskin, 6 . 5 . 0

Metal-gilt 8-day Clock, with
hand-painted Ivory Dial.
Size 4 inches square.
9 . 10 . 0

Silver-gilt and Enamel 8-day Minute
Repeating Clock.
Size 3½ × 2⅝ × 1½ ins.   28 . 10 . 0

Shagreen Hair Brush, with Ivory Comb.
3 . 7 . 6

Gold ½ - Hunter
Watch, in Patent
Swing Opening
Dustproof case.
12 . 10 . 0

Revolving
Mahogany
Poker Chip
Stand.
Fitted with
Paranoid
Chips.
Small
9 . 0 . 0
Large
10 . 15 . 0

Hide Leather
Flat base Handbag.
Size 9 × 6 ins.,   2 . 17 . 6
In various colours.

Mulberry Crocodile Handbag Pochette
Size 8 × 5¾ ins.   6 . 0 . 0

Combined Vanity and Jewel Case,
with Enamelled Silver-gilt Fittings.
13 . 17 . 6

SUITABLE
CHRISTMAS
PRESENTS.

Shagreen
Cigarette Box, Ivory
angled, elevator action.
From 3 . 12 . 6

WRITE FOR
CATALOGUE.

Crocodile Attaché
Case.
From 10 . 5 . 0

Above As it became increasingly acceptable for women to apply cosmetics in public, the handbag was replaced by the vanity case. Like its counterpart, the powder compact, it was richly embellished. This one by Lacloche Frères, 1926, is gold, with black jadeite and black-backed chalcedony; the lid is set with diamonds, lapis lazuli, turquoise, malachite, rhodonite, mother-of-pearl and pearl.

Opposite American film star Joan Crawford in a publicity shot at the beginning of her long career. The original caption reads: 'Joan Crawford, the lovely Metro Goldwyn Mayer player has at last found a very handy device for carrying one's lipstick and perfume vial without losing or breaking them. The handle of her purse is a hollow tube into one end of which the lipstick is held and in the other the perfume vial.'

Style Influences

Dresses that were mere slips of fabric, in a neutral palette of various shades of shimmering pastels, were the perfect backdrop for the dramatic accessory. Boldly abstract jewellery, long cigarette holders, fans, feather boas and the clutch bag all brought fashion to life. The clutch bag was the ideal canvas on which to showcase the decorative styles of the decade; its streamlined modernism made other bags appear over-designed and fussy. Fashioned from new materials such as Bakelite and Perspex, the long narrow rectangular shape had softened corners, replicating the aerodynamic design of the age of speed.

As the decade progressed, the clutch bag evolved into the pochette. While still retaining the rectangular shape of the clutch, some now had the addition of a small handle at the top or back, through which the fingers could slip. Others closed with an envelope flap, either angled to one side or covering the whole bag, which provided a perfect space for the fractional, faceted shapes and sweeping curves of the Cubist-inspired Art Deco movement.

The Art Deco style began in Europe in the early years of the twentieth century, though it was not universally popular until the 1925 *Exposition Internationale des Arts Décoratifs et Industriels Modernes*, and fell out of favour in the late 1930s and 1940s. It was a confluence of many trends, from the arts of Africa, Egypt and Mexico to the streamlined technology and materials of the 'speed age' – from modern aviation and the growing ubiquity of the motorcar. These design influences were expressed in the fractional forms of Cubism and Futurism. The popular motifs of the period – stepped forms, sun-ray motifs, chevron patterns and zigzags – were easily translated into leather, suede or embroidered and appliquéd fabric designs. Exotic materials, such as sharkskin (shagreen) and zebraskin were also favoured.

The discovery of Tutankhamun's tomb in 1922 provoked a craze for ancient Egyptian styles of ornament that endured well into the 1930s. It was an event that held a fascination with the public, fuelled by newsreel footage of archaeological digs and press reports. Howard Carter's remark on peering into the tomb for the first time, that he could see 'marvellous things', heralded an obsession with all things Egyptian, from scarabs, snakes and pyramids to hieroglyphs and sphinxes. The French jeweller Cartier relished the opportunity for Art Deco decadence, with their handbag clasps of pavé diamonds, lapis lazuli and gold scarabs mounted on plain black bags.

Above The simplicity of shape of these two rectangular embroidered purses by the Austrian Hilde Wagner-Ascher in 1925 makes them a perfect canvas to express the geometric forms and patterning of modern art.

Opposite A gold felt bag with hieroglyphic motifs from 1920. A craze for Egyptian-style ornamentation was a feature that carried on into the 1930s. It was sparked by the excavations into the pharaohs' tombs, particularly Tutankhamun's in 1922.

Below Intimations of the Art Deco movement in this green tooled-leather handbag from 1929.

Above Animal skins, such as the snakeskin used to make up this afternoon bag, were popular during the 1920s. The size and scale of the skin are perfectly balanced against the finesse of the chain and the cornelian clasp.

Right Egyptian-themed 1920s beaded bag with a metal 'elephant' clasp and fringing.

Art and the Artisan

The applied arts flourished in the late nineteenth century and first decades of the twentieth century. The Wiener Werkstätte, the Vienna Workshop of 1903–32, was a huge influence on pattern design during this period. With its roots in the Arts and Crafts Movement, the studio progressed from producing exclusive furnishing fabrics to gradually introducing a broader range of products, including bags. Usually created from dark hand-crafted leather with gold tooled patterns, their designs eventually shifted away from the curvilinear forms of Art Nouveau to embrace the more formal stylization of Art Deco, described in embossed and coloured leathers.

Fashion and art were inextricably linked for the Ukrainian artist Sonia Delaunay. Together with her husband, Robert Delaunay, she was a significant pioneer of abstraction. Through her 'colour rhythm' paintings, first shown in 1921, the artist endeavoured to provoke a simultaneous response to form, colour and movement. She produced 'simultaneous' dresses printed with patterns of loosely painted geometric blocks of contrasting colours, which she described as 'colour scales'. In 1927, Sonia Delaunay spoke of 'The Influence of Painting on the Art of Clothes' at the Sorbonne in Paris:

A movement is now influencing fashion, just as it influences interior decoration, the cinema, and all the visual arts … we are only at the beginning of the study of these new colour relationships, still full of mystery to unravel, which are at the base of a modern vision.

The angular abstraction and solid blocks of colour of her work provided an ideal way to decorate the flat planes and angles of a clutch bag: it was a perfect synthesis of form and decoration, and it was perfectly in tune with the era.

A more spontaneous approach to colour was to be found in the work of the avant-garde artists of the time, including a group of French painters called the Fauves ('Wild Beasts'), known for their uncontrolled use of violent, brilliant colour. One of these artists, Raoul Dufy, was introduced to a career in textile design by the couturier Paul Poiret, and from 1912 to 1928, he created more than 2,000 textile designs for the French silk-weaving company Bianchini-Férier. Dufy's strong graphic style, which was evidence of his earlier practice of wood engraving, encompassed a wide range of design genres including narrative, figurative and abstract. His textiles found their way into handbags that had a particular appeal to the 1930s bohemian set.

Above 'Fine art' bags with subjects such as romantic rural landscapes in woven tapestry panels were attractive to the bohemian, together with craft-based jewellery and beaded and embroidered garments, as seen in the two women modelling drop-waisted dresses and suits in 1924.

Opposite An advertisement for Asprey handbags that appeared in *Tatler* magazine in 1926. It features popular styles of the day, including Aubusson tapestry pieces depicting floral arrangements and scenes, a black embroidered silk purse, a leather bag with marcasite and onyx mount and one with a green enamel mount.

This page French couturier Coco Chanel revolutionized women's dress with the introduction of easy tailoring and knitted jersey separates that acknowledged the importance of healthy pursuits such as sea bathing and sport, activities previously confined to men. For the first time it was fashionable to have a suntan and pursue outdoor activities such as golf. Here golfing accessories, including a black-and-white plaid golf bag and a small 'zipper' bag to match, dating from 1929.

Coco Chanel

The understated clothes of the Parisian couturier Coco Chanel (1883–1971) revolutionized modern 1920s fashion. The inventor of the little black dress, she also brought a new, relaxed elegance to informal clothes. Influenced by the sporting garb of her aristocratic English lover, the Duke of Westminster, she popularized the cardigan and the use of wool jersey in a subtle colour palette of navy, taupe and cream, and introduced trousers into her collections. This relaxed, informal approach to fashion also applied to the handbag. She reportedly told her friend Claude Delay that because she was 'sick and tired of holding my handbags and losing them, I stuck a strap on them and wore them across my shoulder'. She was inspired by the military satchel to produce a version of the shoulder bag. Her first styles in 1929 were made from black or navy jersey, and lined in red or blue grosgrain.

This design evolved into one of the most significant fashion items of the twentieth century, the 2.55 bag, named for the month and the year of its creation, and requiring 180 different processes in its manufacture. Inspired by the checked shirts of racetrack stable boys, the quilted jersey or leather bag hung from a long gold chain interlaced with leather, and featured a rectangular gold-plated lock. The interlocked-Cs logo was stitched onto the lining. Three flap pockets made up its solid, rectangular shape: the first in the shape of a tube for lipstick, the second zipped and the third for papers and letters.

During the 1920s, Coco Chanel was one of the first couturiers to realize the potential of accessories as a way to increase sales. Accordingly, she opened a boutique in her Paris salon that was dedicated to accessories and jewellery. Couturiers such as Jean Patou, Jeanne Lanvin and Mainbocher, while not specializing in handbag design, added to the total look of an outfit by designing matching clutches.

Left Versions of the most iconic bag ever, the Chanel 2.55, so named for the month and year of its inception. The 2.55 had its provenance in the quilted jersey shoulder bag that was inspired by the military satchel of the First World War, which Chanel first devised in 1929.

Above Dressing the modern woman. At last freed from the corset and the hobble skirt, Chanel designed clothes in 1929 of wearable simplicity to a formula that has contemporary resonances in the simple edge-to-edge jacket and knee-length skirt. The handbag seen here is equally timeless.

New Materials and Technology

The machine age brought innovation and the invention of new materials. It was inevitable that these would infiltrate fashion from their architectural or product-design origins. Plastics were one of the most significant cultural phenomena of the twentieth century. They changed the way objects were designed, produced and used; their chief quality was their ability to be moulded or shaped into different forms under pressure or by heat. Plastics revolutionized the injection-moulding process, which remains one of the primary ways to manufacture them.

After the arrival of the first plastics, such as celluloid in 1868, casein in 1897 and cellulose acetate in 1926, it became possible to imitate expensive natural raw materials, such as horn, tortoiseshell and ivory. The plastic simulation of these substances enabled bag manufacturers to produce more affordable ranges for the average woman. Eventually, plastics came to be used for their own properties rather than as faux animal products; one example is the fluorescent cellulose acetate that went under the trade name Rhodoid.

Bakelite was invented by the Belgian chemist Leo Baekeland in 1905. Once the patents on the product had expired in 1927, it pervaded all aspects of product design, and was embraced enthusiastically by handbag designers who loved its malleability and bright colours. It was formed by the reaction under heat and pressure of phenol (a toxic, colourless crystalline solid) and formaldehyde (a simple organic compound), and was the first plastic to be made from synthetic components. Initially, Bakelite was used for its electrically nonconductive and heat-resistant properties in electrical insulators, hence its connotations with old-fashioned brown radios and household electrical goods. However, its properties made Bakelite an excellent bearer of the stylized forms found in Art Deco, and it soon came to be associated with lively handbag design. Bandalasta, also known as Lingalonga, was a colourful marbled version of Bakelite that appeared in 1925.

Shagreen, a type of untanned leather, was also typical of the era, and used for many designed objects as well as handbags. Made from sharkskin, its distinctive surface comes from the shark's round, calcified papillae (called placoid scales), which were ground down to give a roughened surface of rounded protrusions; the dye, which is typically green vegetable dye, shows between these protrusions when the skin is coloured from the other side. Although the process was invented during the eighteenth century by Jean-Claude Galluchat, it was the British artisan John Paul Cooper who developed the technique in his London studio between 1899 and 1933.

Below An ornate French evening bag dating from 1920–30, constructed in ribbed shot silk in gold and black. The plastic frame is embossed with coloured flowers and foliage, and inscribed 'Depose'. The press closure is also decorated with an embossed and coloured floral knob, with a matching single chain handle, and the edge is trimmed with leaf-shaped pendants. The front plaque has a round mirror on the underside and is positioned to cover a small pocket opening.

Above left Moulded plastic was frequently used for handbag 'hardware' during the 1920s and '30s. This clutch bag, quilted and corded in a geometric design in black satin, has a covered brass frame with an Art Deco bar clasp of moulded plastic sections in light green and black. The bag features an internal silk coin purse with a twist knob closure on a central pivot.

Left A 1928 selection of handbags from the Revelation Suitcase Company. Although the products are described as 'not necessarily expensive', the antelope bag cost £21.0.0 – a month's wages for an office worker.

Collectable Mesh Bags

'Truly, a Whiting & Davis Mesh bag is the very embodiment of queenly beauty, refinement and utility,' said the *Ladies' Home Journal* in December 1923. The popularity of the ring mesh bag increased during the 1920s and 1930s with the introduction of Armor (armour) mesh, a flat surface formed by four-armed mesh cells or 'spiders' linked by rings at each corner. Previously, the mesh bag had been restricted to the use of silver and golden threads, but this new construction was ideal for the technique of enamelling, which enabled the application of the vibrant colour palette that was such an essential element of the handbag during this period. Paul Poiret was one of the designers commissioned to work for the company, his rainbow palette and distinctive Oriental patterning adding interest to the lustrous folds of the mesh bag. The American version of Art Deco, which was cleaner and more streamlined than the European style, lent itself to the medium of mesh; it provided vortices of blazing colour, interspersed with heavy black lines typical of the era. In contrast, the extremely fine Dresden mesh or baby-ring mesh was ideal for the gauzy, multicoloured pictorial imagery of abstract design, which was stencilled to the surface in muted colours in a form of screen printing.

Manufacturing processes dictated the parameters of the mesh bag and the squared-off, boxy shape; 12.5 x 25 cm (5 x 10 inches) was deemed appropriate for optimum practicality. Variety was introduced by cutting the base of the bag into various shapes, the most popular being the Vandyke, with triangular points repeated in various scales and lengths. Novelty also came from the diverse trimmings deployed. Fringing was the most popular, and sometimes incorporated metal drops, which came in various shapes: the round teardrop, the ovoid and the bullet. One style of fringing was the Venetian fringe, containing a central rosette, patented in 1923. Clasps, too, were an opportunity to change the style of the bag, and variations included the standard ball and socket, twist-knob clasps, and side-mounted latches. The 1920s also saw the popularity of 'dome' or 'cathedral' frames, which were decorated with jewels, embossed or enamelled. Vermeil was a gold-tone mesh of silver gilt.

Beadlite was a variation of Armor mesh: a raised dot in the centre of each 'spider' was enamelled, creating the tromp l'oeil effect of a beaded bag. The mesh could also be coated with an iridescent glaze, called Fishscale. Aluminium was used in the 1930s under the name Alu-mesh.

Whiting & Davis handbags

The Whiting & Davis logo, first used in 1921, became a registered trademark in 1922, appearing on shield-shaped paper tags (blue for soldered mesh, white for all other mesh). This was followed by a metal tag attached to the bag frame. Finally, the logo was stamped on the inner side of the metal frame.

Opposite above and below An early twentieth-century example of a gold metal mesh bag attached to a curved metal frame with a twist knob closure and single chain handle. The fastening is bud-shaped and is inset with blue glass. The scalloped edge is formed by a pale blue flower bud braid.

It is important for the collector to make sure that the mesh and the fringing are intact, and that there is no damage to either the frame or any embellishment. Torn linings are less of a problem, as these can be replaced without reducing the value of the bag. Original bags should be cleaned with a fine, soft brush and stored separately from each other, away from bright, strong sunlight. It is important to remember when buying a Whiting & Davis vintage bag that their bags are still being produced.

Features to look for in vintage mesh bags

- Bags with a fringe and drops, or indeed both, as they are more expensive.
- Bags made of finer mesh, such as baby-ring mesh.
- Any additional decoration on the clasp, particularly those of precious metals or jewels used in the bag's construction.
- Clear and unfaded images, especially on the Dresden type.
- Multipurpose bags such as vanity or 'function' bags.
- Bags that have retained their packaging, receipt and original labels.
- Pure silver bags tend to be lighter for their size, with smaller rings, than those made of base metal. American silver bags are usually marked 'sterling'; European ones are stamped 'silver' or have a hallmark.

Below The look of
needlework is re-created in
mesh on this ornate and
highly coloured bag with
stepped fringe and decorative
metal frame by French
company Breville, dating
from the 1920s.

Right The handbag
coordinates perfectly with the
cloche hat and day dress by
Maison Gerda, circa 1925.

Mandalian bags

The main competitor of Whiting & Davis for the mesh bag market was the Mandalian Manufacturing Company, founded in 1915 by Turkish-born Sahatiel G Mandalian. His Eastern aesthetic influenced the design of the bags, in contrast with those of the rival company. Whereas Whiting & Davis exploited the abstract geometric forms of Art Deco, Mandalian bags featured exotic, intricate patterning reminiscent of Persian carpets, ornate gardens, luscious roses, peacocks and feathers in rich, deep colours. These details were enhanced with a shimmering surface, the result of the Lustro-Pearl effect, a process of coating the enamel with a solution of 'essence of pearl' that gave an iridescent finish to the bags. Trimmings were equally lush and ornate, incorporating bejewelled frames and clasps, and Byzantine-like tiers of drops and fringing. Mandalian bags differed from their competitor's because the mesh cells were set on the diagonal, whereas the majority of Whiting & Davis bags had the mesh placed on horizontal and vertical lines. The company also developed the use of smaller 'spiders' to create a finer mesh surface. Mandalian specialities included the Gloria bag, featuring a bracelet frame; its spring-joined links formed a roomy, box-like opening. In 1944, the Mandalian Manufacturing Company was absorbed by Whiting & Davis.

Left A form of screen printing allowed for the application of surface decoration on mesh bags in the 1920s, as is the case with this fine metal mesh bag printed in shades of green, yellow, lilac and coral pink. The base of the bag has an indented fringe trim. The square gilt frame is engraved with scrolling foliage to which a gilt chain handle is attached. The twist knob closure is tipped in black plastic or glass.

Jazz Age Jewellery

Opposite A Cartier necklace and matching earrings in emeralds and pearls create Modernist elegance in 1924. The Art Deco dress pin and cabochon headband were re-interpreted by many fine and costume jewellers.

Modernism transformed the look of the twentieth century arising like a phoenix from the ashes of the First World War to sweep away both the febrile swirls of Art Nouveau and the Rococo tracery of High Edwardian style. The first generation born in the twentieth century felt a deep-seated need to reject the cult of the past and the revivalist styles of jewellery that they associated with their parents. Modernism was clearly the appropriate aesthetic for the age of the machine: hard-edged, clean-cut and pared down to purity.

Such innovation of line and form first surfaced in the architecture of Adolf Loos in Vienna and Le Corbusier in France. Loos was garrulous in his antipathy to any overly decorative form in design, intoning, 'Ornament is Crime' in his polemical writings. He continued, 'We are approaching a new and greater time. No longer by an appeal to sensuality, but rather by economic dependence earned through work, will women bring about her equal status with man. Then velvet, silk and ribbons, feathers and paint will fail to have their effect. They will disappear.'

Fashion did undergo a transformation, but perhaps not as radically as Loos would have liked, and the more youthful streamlined garçonne silhouette – with its dropped waist, perfect for showing off long strings of beads, sleeveless shift dresses and shortened skirts – reflected the new opportunities for women that were emerging professionally, socially and politically. The new woman or 'flapper', as the popular press dubbed her, had hair newly bobbed or shorn into an Eton crop, all the better for showing off a pair of huge drop earrings in ivory or Cubist cloisonné. Such 'bright young things' made the old sartorial rules redundant; softly dimpled faces no longer flirted behind fans but were vividly painted, scarlet red lips drawn into a Cupid's bow amid lashings of stark white face powder. Socialite and novelist Violet Trefusis, daughter of Alice Keppel (the mistress of Edward VII) and lover of Vita Sackville-West, wrote of the new 'brittle' goddesses with 'bones of joss sticks, eyes by Fabergé and hearts made out of Venetian glass' such as the fictitious character Terpsichore van Pusch, who wore 'a hat with two little mercury wings specifically designed for her by Lucienne', with matching diamond wings on her ears.

Art and Industry

The actual application of Modernist principles to smaller-scale design took place at the Bauhaus, a German design school that operated from 1919 onwards under the auspices of director Walter Gropius, its influence continuing even when the school was forcibly shut by Hitler's Nazi forces in 1933. The Bauhaus philosophy of 'form follows function' was applied to all the products emanating from this influential think-tank of avant-garde teachers and students. Bauhaus design had to have a 'fitness for purpose' and found visual expression in pure ergonomic lines, such as in the tubular steel and canvas chair by Marcel Breuer, a clear break from the overstuffed comfort and cosy domesticity of the traditional fireside seat, and the glass and steel Constructivist tables by Modernist visionary Ludwig Mies van der Rohe.

The Bauhaus instigated a radical concept into the designer's oeuvre – designing for industry. William Morris had proposed the unification of art and design but his ideas were essentially romantic and small-scale, and no amount of lovingly crafted pseudo Gothic objects created in medieval-inspired guilds and workshops could meet the demands of a world hungry for cheap consumer durables. The Bauhaus was an urban operation embracing the world of industrial processes and mass production, seeing industry as the utopian route to good design in every home. The romantic and aesthetic complexities of nineteenth-century Art Nouveau were also to be wholly rejected in favour of a style of design based on bare essentials. Life was now being lived too fast for any bourgeois visual distraction.

Naum Slutzky

Born in Kiev to goldsmith Gilel Slutzky, Naum (1894–1965) trained in Vienna under the jeweller Anton Dumant before working for a short time at the Wiener Werkstätte in 1912. After studying engineering, he was invited by Walter Gropius to join the Bauhaus at its inception as assistant in the metal and goldsmithing workshops, where he became master goldsmith in 1922. His jewellery designs in steel and brass are an extreme embodiment of Bauhaus philosophy; monastic in their austerity, every unnecessary detail is stripped away to leave an almost elemental elegance – reinforced with the complete refusal to apply any historical references. Slutzky's work may appear simple yet it is superbly engineered, instantly recognizable by its futuristic use of steel with a gleaming chromium finish. Bracelets and neckpieces have an abstract geometry that relates to the visual language of the Russian Constructivists and the De Stijl group, in particular the planar play of architect and furniture designer Gerrit Rietveld's Red Blue chair of 1923. When the Bauhaus closed, Slutzky moved to England, where he became professor of industrial design at Ravensbourne College of Art.

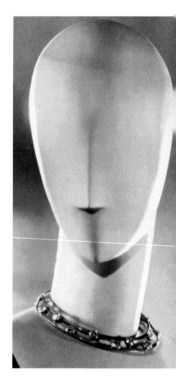

Above Jean Fouquet used loosely twisted bands of 'grey' gold to create a collar, scattered with diamonds that appear to orbit around the neck. It was created in 1928 for Princess Jean-Louis de Faucigny-Lucinge – friend of Salvador Dalí.

Opposite Pure, pared-down Modernism in jewellery design was seen at its most austere in the work of Naum Slutzky at the Bauhaus in the 1920s. He fashioned this pendant necklace from chromium-plated brass tubing.

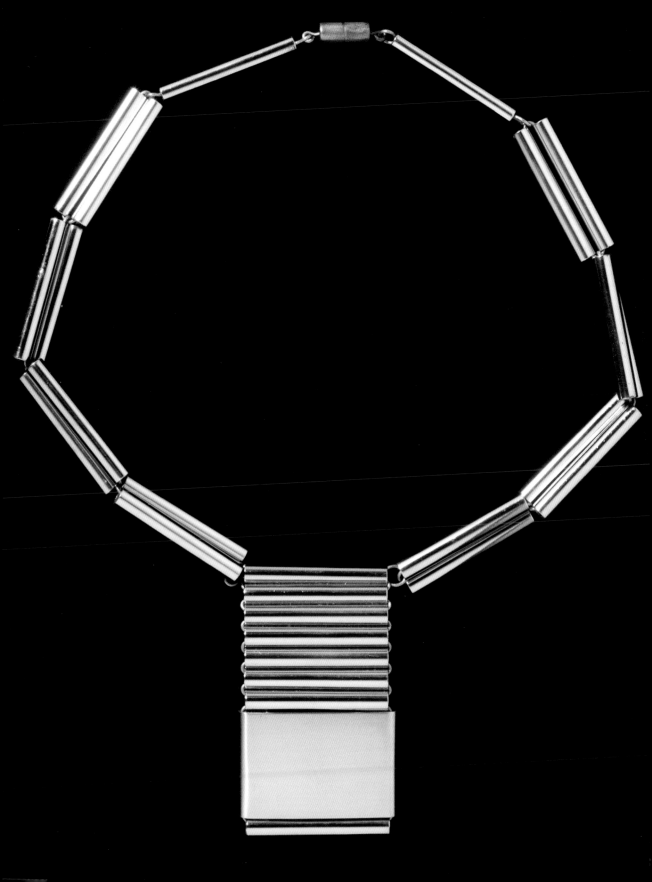

THE RISE OF THE GEMSTONE

By the 1920s Bauhaus Modernism had infiltrated jewellery; a significant moment occurred when the institution Fouquet & Sons refitted in a controlled, sleekly modern style. French jewellers Cartier and Boucheron injected a more palatable glamour into the originally austere Bauhaus style and the Exposition Internationale des Arts Décoratifs held in Paris in 1925 popularized this new French deluxe version of Bauhaus Modernism to an international audience. Its huge jewellery pavilion in the Grand Palais showcased work by Aucoc, Boucheron, Van Cleef & Arpels and Mauboussin, among other fine houses, all set against draperies of the palest dusky-rose crepe de chine.

Geometric settings were given a deluxe high-end feel with huge gemstones to create *joaillerie* – jewellery that focused on high-impact gemstones rather than Art Nouveau *bijouterie* with its emphasis on metalwork. New advances in machine rather than hand-cutting, such as the rectangular-shaped baguette, gave gems a sharper line and edge that complemented the geometric Deco settings. Large citrines, amethysts and chunks of rock crystal found favour during this period, their translucency played against opaque materials such as coral and jade – and the juxtaposition of a diamond set against onyx gave a stark visual contrast in monochrome black that seemed an absolute fit with the dynamic feel of the times. Hematite, the principal ore of iron was used for its hard metallic shine. Its dark crystal formations complemented the polished surface of silver and grey gold or super-shiny black lacquer, particularly stunning in the work of Raymond Templier. Clashing shades of emerald and tango, inspired by the Ballets Russes of 1909–29, also enjoyed a vogue among the bohemian set in Paris. The opening of Tutankhamun's tomb in 1922 led to a mania for Egyptian motifs such as winged scarabs and pharaoh's heads – the Castellani workshop in Rome was famed for its luxurious interpretations of the ancient Egyptian style.

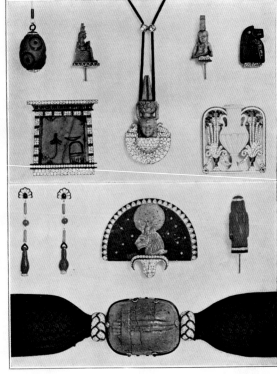

EGYPTIAN TRINKETS FROM 1500 TO 3000 YEARS OLD ADAPTED AS MODERN JEWELLERY: BROOCHES, PENDANTS, EARRINGS, AND HAT-PINS SET WITH REAL ANTIQUES, AND A TUTANKHAMEN REPLICA.

Above The discovery of Tutankhamun's tomb in 1922 created a short-lived craze for Egyptian-style jewellery. Cartier went one step further by setting brooches, pendants, earrings and hatpins with ancient Egyptian artefacts.

Opposite The magnificent jewellery pavilion at the *Exposition Internationale des Arts Décoratifs* in Paris, 1925, introduced the key names of French Art Deco design to an international audience.

This page The romance of the machine and the speed and dynamism of modern metropolitan life were reflected in 1920s jewellery design. A ring by Alexandre Marchak of Paris, circa 1920–30, combines platinum with coral, diamonds and innovative black plastic, right, while a gold and chrome ring set with diamonds by Jean Desprès, circa 1930, is achieved in the ball-bearing style, below.

The Machine Aesthetic

The jewellers associated with French Art Deco include Jean Fouquet, Gérard Sandoz, Suzanne Belperron and Raymond Templier – all of whose work experimented with the basic geometry of circles, the smooth surfaces of squares and sharp-edged rectangles reflecting the general vogue for what design historian Bevis Hillier dubbed 'domesticated Cubism'. Raymond Templier made full use of the chevron, a particularly popular shape in Art Deco jewellery, having originally appeared on the canvases of the Italian Futurists who were operating as an avant-garde group in the cities of Milan and Turin just before the First World War.

Speed transfixed these Italian mavericks, conveyed pictorially by the use of sequenced diagonals, planes, angles and interpenetrating forms. Artist Giacomo Balla, in particular, used the chevron to convey a sense of wonder at the technology that was changing the world, such as the 1909 electrification of Milan in *Street Light* (1909–10), a painting in which multicoloured chevrons are used to depict the dynamism of a street lamp's cosmic glow. The machine aesthetic can also be seen in the paintings of Tamara de Lempicka, who painted a self-portrait in 1929 that is the epitome of Art Deco glamour: the artist as a heavy-lidded Russian émigré posed in a shiny green Bugatti racing car with leather gloves, a metallic leather driving cap and a billowing scarf. The perfect woman for Jean Fouquet, for instance, who began to design bulkier rings in the 1920s using frosted rock crystal, cabochon moonstones and faceted amethysts set into platinum, correctly believing that 'the female hand holding the steering wheel would not be able to adorn itself with too fragile a ring.'

This glamorous modern woman would surely have been the customer for the most extreme examples of machine-inspired style such as the jewellery constructed out of ball bearings by Charlotte Perriand, Jean Després and Gérard Sandoz. Ball bearings were commonly used to eliminate friction in mechanical parts, specifically axles, and took the form of simple chromium-plated brass balls – a fabulous shape for invention. These perfect silver spheres were threaded onto lengths of steel or copper wire to make the most Modernist of necklaces and sautoirs (a type of long necklace with a pendant or tassel hanging from the end) or were trapped between cases of ebonite and displayed on the arm. It would have taken a woman of great presence to wear this kind of jewellery when her contemporaries complacently flashed their diamonds. In 1920, film star and celebrated bisexual Marlene Dietrich was spotted in a silver bracelet created by Cartier that was decorated with small gold spheres in the ball-bearing style – reputedly a present from her lover, Jean Gabin.

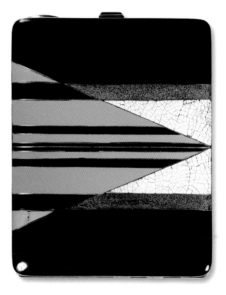

Below An enamelled and lacquered silver cigarette case by Art Deco jeweller Gérard Sandoz takes the dynamic angles of Futurism and converts them into an *objet de luxe*.

THE BARBARIC BANGLE

Each decade has an item of covetable jewellery that chimes with the times and resonates with the stylistic credo of the era. There is always a hierarchy of desire – for particular items of jewellery may not be equally in vogue. It was the bangle, a rigid circle that could be fashioned out of materials from precious metal to the more prosaic Bakelite, which achieved unprecedented heights of popularity in the 1920s. Emancipated flappers – the seductive sirens of new Jazz Age – were no longer fettered with corsets and ostentatiously dressed hair. Freed from the constraints and restrictions of the pre-war Edwardian period, the bangle became the ultimate expression of modernity.

Much Deco jewellery referenced the geometry found in the paintings of Pablo Picasso and Georges Braque. Protagonists of one of the most influential art movements of the twentieth century, these iconic Cubist artists were profoundly influenced by the formal simplification and expressive power of African sculpture, clearly expressed in Picasso's *Les Demoiselles d'Avignon* (1907), in which the women appear to be wearing African masks. Within intellectual circles in Paris, collecting African art was extremely fashionable and African culture seen as a paradigm of a life lived free from the constraints of a dull and bourgeois society. Some members of the European avant-garde went even further, appropriating aspects of African dress, including the wearing of African-inspired jewellery – Jean Dunand's giraffe multi-ringed necklaces in red and black lacquered gold were all the rage. Josephine Baker, a dancer who wowed Paris in *La Revue Nègre*, exemplified the popularity of this style. On stage she performed stripped to the waist with glossy brilliantined black hair by celebrity coiffeur Antoine de Paris and flashed huge, lacquered cuff bracelets by Jean Dunand.

Opposite An illustration from the fashion magazine *Le Gazette du Bon Ton* by Georges Barbier shows the rampant appropriation of global culture inherent in 1920s fashion; the 'barbaric' colour palette of red and green from Africa and arm of 'tribal' cuffs and bangles is mixed with a Japanese floral arrangement and a French Rococo table.

Below The bangle has become a ubiquitous symbol of the 1920s, a simple Modernist loop that could be fashioned out of a variety of materials and matched the freedom of contemporary fashion. Like Picasso and Braque before him, sculptor and designer Jean Dunand found inspiration in African culture, as seen in this lacquered brass bangle from 1925.

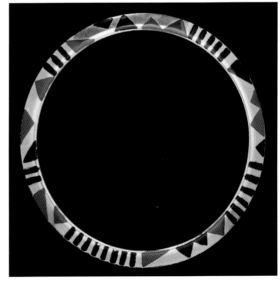

GEORGE BARBIER 1925

Jean Dunand

Swiss-born Dunand (1877–1942) was an
accomplished sculptor who had studied at the
School of Industrial Arts in Geneva, travelling to Paris
as a scholarship student around the turn of the
twentieth century. Here he worked as an apprentice
to the sculptor Jean Dampt for five years and was
encouraged by his mentor to realize his ambition to
become an interior designer. It was in *dinanderie*
that Dunand really found his forte; the name given
to work in brass derived from the Flemish city of
Dinant, which had been an important centre for the
production of this type of metalwork in the fifteenth
century. Dunand's *dinanderie* caught the attention
of the critics in 1905 when he exhibited three softly
hammered-brass vases at the Salon la Nationale.
One review at the time ran: 'This brilliant artist seems
to have drawn from copper all that this metal has to
offer by way of full and subtle form.'

In 1912, once he had learnt the techniques
of Japanese lacquer from artist Seizo Sugawara
and recognized how such skills could be used to
enhance the work he had been producing in wood
and metal, his career really took off. He collaborated
with the great furniture designer Emile-Jacques
Ruhlmann to apply luxurious lacquer finishes in a Cubo-Japanese style to his
designs and was a successful creator of a whole series of stunning Art Deco
lacquered screens. One of Dunand's most important commissions was for the
interior of the first-class dining room of the great ocean liner *Alantique* in 1930
and panels for the smoking room of the *Normandie* in 1935. It was not long
before Dunand was applying his experimental lacquer techniques to jewellery,
such as metal buckles and clips, an interest sparked off in the 1920s by his
friendship with the couturier Madeleine Vionnet, for whom he produced a
lacquered panel depicting three panthers, a popular 1920s motif.

Dunand's Art Deco jewellery is created from copper inlaid with silver or
combinations of lacquered wood and metal. One of his most distinctive stylistic
devices is a striking chequerboard effect, most commonly of red and silver, that
manages to combine the pure lines of Modernism with an uninhibited 'barbaric'
luxury. Huge metal Cubist earrings recall the thrusting New York skyscraper and
his trademark bracelets are fashioned from huge rectangular metal plaques,
big enough to serve as a micro-canvas for a miniature Cubist painting and
joined together with sturdy rings or hinges. Rigid bangles and cuffs are moulded
from nickel, copper and brass, and lacquered with Cubist patterns.

Shipping heiress Nancy Cunard (1895–1965) personified the flamboyant
excess of Dunand's look. Born in 1896 to an American mother and an English

Above Heiress, poet
and political activist
Nancy Cunard poses in
her trademark outsized
African ivory bangles that
stretch from elbow to wrist,
and a huge 'barbaric'
wooden necklace.

baronet, she frequented the cafes of Paris with her 'corrupt coterie' of fellow bohemians – Iris Tree, Osbert Sitwell, Ezra Pound and Augustus John. In 1928 she founded Hours Press, which published writers such as George Moore, Samuel Beckett and Robert Graves. Her long and languid form and etiolated limbs, emphasized by the newly bobbed and shorn hair, required a different type of jewellery. She adopted the wearing of outsize African ivory bangles that stretched from elbow to wrist on both arms or Cubist cuff bracelets to express her solidarity with black struggles against social injustice. To achieve such a performance of rather patronizing 'primitivism', she was reputed to own several lacquered abstract designs by Dunand that she wore with long necklaces of heavy wooden beads wound around her neck and shimmering scarves wrapped into a turban, anticipating the radical chic of the 1970s.

In 1929 *The New York Times* called these back-to-nature artefacts of wood, bone and ivory 'jewellery for the new barbarians'. In wearing the jewellery Cunard was, by analogy, investing herself with the stereotypical notions of the primitive sexuality of African women. Her relationship with the African-American jazz musician, Henry Crowder, scandalized society and, after being ostracized by her parents, confirmed her status as an outsider. By the early 1930s the so-called 'barbaric' look had lost its avant-garde status and was being produced by many of the high-end jewellery firms. Boucheron, for instance, exhibited a large African cuff bracelet at the Exposition Coloniale in 1931, which combined ivory, green malachite and purpurite, a manganese phosphate mineral with a striking purple colour, interspersed with polished gold beads.

Right American singer and dancer Josephine Baker modelling ornate and chunky diamond jewellery and not much else.

Fashion and Jewellery Combine

The links between the houses of fashion and jewellery have always been eminently exploitable. Louis Cartier, the man at the helm of the Paris-based jewellers in the early twentieth century, married Andrée Worth, daughter of Jean-Philippe Worth and grand-daughter of Charles Frederick Worth, the grande couturier.

Another link in the proverbial chain was forged when jeweller René Boivin married couturier Paul Poiret's sister Jeanne. It was in the 1920s, however, when clearer collaborations were cleverly marketed to the haute-couture crowd. Several fashion houses and jewellery firms joined forces to display their wares; in 1927, Jean Patou showed dresses accessorized with the colour-matched jewels of Georges Fouquet (significantly both names had equal prominence in the programme) and in 1931, Jeanne Lanvin showed with Boucheron.

Left This 1924 illustration is a modern take on the Judgement of Paris from classical mythology. Fashion and jewellery are perfectly matched as long strings and circlets of pearls offset the pale draped satin of the evening gowns. The centre gown incorporates jewellery in its construction.

Opposite A sleeveless satin draped dress by couturier Jean Patou, accessorized by a triple strand of pearls and a large turquoise pin in the Egyptian style by Fouquet, circa 1928.

Coco Chanel and costume jewellery

It was not long before astute designers realized they could parley out their brands by applying their own name to branded jewellery that would provide a direct visual link with their couture gowns. Coco Chanel, always a canny operator, understood the power of her moniker after the unmitigated success of what was dubbed her 'poverty de luxe' look. The understated chic of Coco's little black dress moved the language of fashion from the vulgar and showy to something a little more sophisticated and harder to define, a must for the more discerning post-war customer who wanted to distance themselves from the Edwardian past. Fashion was no longer about the overt flashing of cash; it was about being to able to navigate your way as a modern woman in the city without being seen as a rich man's plaything or a mere working girl. The colour black had formerly only been used for mourning dress; Chanel made it elegant and wearable anyplace, any time. The simple, uncluttered lines of a garment of such stream-lined efficiency (almost the sartorial equivalent of the Ford motor car) was also a perfect background to jewellery and it was here that Chanel hit upon a groundbreaking idea. She cast aside the use of real gemstones substituting the much cheaper glass in their place. Her explanation? 'Because they were devoid of arrogance in an atmosphere of too-easy luxe.'

In one fell swoop Coco kickstarted the whole trend for what became known as costume jewellery. From 1921, Chanel boutiques sold pieces in an Art Deco style that appeared somewhat derivative of the other Parisian jewellery firms, but in 1924 showed a breakthrough collection designed with the Maison Gripoix, who were renowned as the leaders in glass jewellery. *Harper's Bazaar* greeted the resultant gems in poured glass as 'the most revolutionary designs of our time' and they were produced in a whole host of styles that ranged from Indian, Baroque and Renaissance to the more obvious Art Deco. The most recognizable piece is the pearl or faux pearl necklace, sometimes interspersed with other metal and crystal beads and the signature use of red and green poured glass, influenced by the Byzantine treasury of St Marks in Venice. The couturier and her models were walking advertisements for this new look, seen at the races or the Bois de Boulogne swathed in ropes and ropes of pearls and glittering gewgaws as a theatrical counterpoint to the simplicity of the clothes. In 1929 Chanel affixed a huge brooch to her beret and the fashion house persuaded other women to follow suit by showing huge gold-tone pins in the shape of Maltese crosses with a faux pearl at the centre and ruby red poured-glass hearts surround by diamanté.

Another of Chanel's innovative ideas was to set fabulous gems in informal settings, a result of her collaboration with designer Duke Fulco di Verdura. The Duke of Westminster, the incalculably wealthy lover of Chanel, who was described by diarist Sir Henry Channon as a 'mixture of Henry VIII and Lorenzo Il Magnifico', had reputedly given Chanel some precious stones and she had asked Fulco what she should do with them. He had responded with a languorous, 'The thought of designing something for all these different stones is *too* enervating,' and his solution was to treat the precious gems with simplicity

Above In 1929, Coco Chanel pinned a huge brooch to her beret and thousands of women followed suit. Here she sports the same look in 1937, together with swathes of pearls and a Maltese Cross cuff by Fulco di Verdura.

rather than showiness – as if they were mere baubles. Fulco's design comprised a single chain containing all the different coloured stones in restrained understatement, an approach that blurred the boundaries between costume jewellery and 'the real thing'.

Chanel's new approach was irreverent and appeared democratic, but her work was still prohibitively expensive for any woman of standard income. It wasn't until the invention of injection-plastic moulding in 1934 that such brightly coloured pieces could be available to all. Yet it was through Chanel that modern techniques infiltrated the design of precious jewellery, a journey that was to have profound effects in the decade of the Depression, a time when women wanted aspirational fantasies very much on the cheap.

Opposite These summer ensembles, trimmed with grey fox fur, left, and foxaline, a cheaper pelt dyed to resemble fox fur, right, are complemented by simple strands of pearls and beads.

Left Long, multiple strands of pearls and a variety of diamanté bracelets complete the look of this extravagant stage costume.

Coco Chanel talks jewellery

- 'Costume jewellery is not made to give women an aura of wealth, but to make them beautiful.'
- 'If you want to start a collection, start with a brooch because you will find most use for it. It can be pinned on a suit lapel, collar or pocket, on a hat, belt or evening gown.'
- 'My jewellery never stands in isolation from the idea of women and their dress. And because dresses change, so does my jewellery.'
- 'A woman should mix fake and real. To ask a woman to wear real jewellery is only like asking her to cover herself with real flowers instead of flowery silk prints. She'd look faded in a few hours.'
- 'I love fakes because I find such jewellery provocative, and I find it disgraceful to walk around with millions around your neck just because you're rich. The point of jewellery isn't to make a woman look rich but to adorn her; not the same thing.'
- 'I couldn't wear my own pearls without being stopped on the street, so I started the vogue of wearing false ones.'

Above A Murano glass bead necklace in the typically 1920s colour combination of red, black and white, which has its roots in the experimental colour palettes of the Russian Constructivists, Agitprop artists of the Russian Revolution.

Opposite Not all 1920s jewellery is uncompromisingly Modernist in design. Here, a Venetian glass bead necklace shows that the Rococo revival was still popular, especially among more conservative women.

Directory of 1920s Designers

Asprey
Fashionable London jeweller and luxury goods house, founded in 1781 by William Asprey. Its leather, tapestry and silk handbags were particularly popular in the 1920s.

Aucoc, Louis (1850–1932)
French Art Nouveau jeweller and goldsmith.

Belperron, Suzanne (1900–1983)
French jewellery designer who began her career at Boivin where she worked until 1932 when she joined Hertz. She is considered revolutionary for using geometric shapes and combining unusual materials.

Bendel, Henri (1868–1936)
A milliner by trade, American-born Bendel was the first retailer to bring the designs of Coco Chanel to the US, and the founder of his eponymous New York department store.

Boivin, René (1864–1917)
French jeweller, whose firm Boivin produced some of the most original and finely wrought jewels of the twentieth century. Well known for their craftsmanship, modern and sculptural designs, and the use of coloured stones.

Boucheron
French jewellery house, established in Paris in 1858 by Frédéric Boucheron. His son Louis is credited with creating a new style of jewellery based on technological discoveries and accessories for the 'new woman' of the 1920s, such as long earrings to enhance their short hairstyles.

Brown Shoe Company (Buster Brown)
The cartoon character Buster Brown was the name behind the shoe empire created in 1893 in St Louis. Buster Brown's sister, Mary Jane, was immortalized when her name was applied to single-strap children's shoes in 1909. Flappers adopted the style in the 1920s.

Callot Soeurs
The couture houses, founded the four Callot sisters, Marie, Marthe, Regina and Joséphine, opened in 1895. They were among the first designers to use gold and silver lamé for their dresses.

Cartier
French jeweller and watch manufacturer since 1847, with a long history of catering to royalty and affluent clientele and known as the 'jeweller of kings and the king of jewellers'.

Chanel, Coco (1883–1971)
French designer Gabrielle 'Coco' Chanel established the couture house Chanel in 1914, and revolutionized haute couture with her simple tailored suits and twinsets. She is known for her many 'firsts' in fashion, including the 'little black dress' and two-tone shoes.

Després, Jean (1889–1980)
French Art Deco jewellery designer, known for his innovative geometric patterns. He rejected the rules of fine jewellery and the use of precious stones.

Doucet, Jacques (1853–1929)
French fashion designer, known primarily for his elegant dresses made with flimsy, translucent fabrics in superimposing pastel colours.

Dunand, Jean (1877–1942)
Swiss-born metalsmith and lacquer artist, who designed a small but stunning body of Art Deco jewellery. Renowned for his exquisite use of lacquers and enamels.

Dunhill
Prestigious British design house, famous in the 1920s for its leather goods, particularly handbags.

Erté (pseudonym of Romain de Tirtoff) (1892–1990)
Russian-born French artist and designer who excelled in fashion, jewellery, costume and set design, among other things. Famous for his elegant fashion designs that captured the Art Deco period in which he worked. He also designed hundreds of covers for *Harper's Bazaar*.

Fortuny, Mariano (1871–1949)

Spanish-born fabric and clothing designer, forever associated with the famous pleated silk he invented in 1909. His Delphos gown, a long sheath dress that clung to the curves of the body, was styled after the garments of ancient Greece.

Fouquet, Jean (1899–1994)

Designer of highly innovative jewellery, characterized by its simplicity and clear geometric shapes, often in luminous colours and contrasting combinations.

Gallenga, Maria Monaci (1880–1944)

Italian artist turned fashion designer, who drew inspiration from the work of the Pre-Raphaelites. Best known for her medieval and Oriental designs, hand-stencilled in silver and gold.

Heim, Jacques (1899–1967)

French designer, who took over the family business of manufacturing and designing furs in 1923, then extended it into a couture house.

Hellstern & Sons

Parisian shoe emporium founded in 1872 by Louis Hellstern. Under his son Charles, the company became hugely successful in the 1920s, producing T-strap, plain pumps and instep strappy shoes. The shoe shapes were typical of the period but their colour and decoration set them apart.

Holley, Berthe

American designer who devised the concept of interchangeable coordinated separates in order to expand the wardrobe.

Julienne

One of the few female footwear designers of the 1920s, based in Paris, producing outstanding shoes.

Kurzman

Noted high-class New York milliner and dressmaker.

Lacloche Frères

Spanish jewellery company that moved to Paris at the turn of the twentieth century. In the 1920s, it became known for its Art Deco feminine accessories, such as elaborate jewelled vanity and cigarette cases, lipstick holders and powder compacts.

Lanvin, Jeanne (1867–1946)

A trained milliner, Lanvin established the fashion house Lanvin in Paris in 1885. Famous for her romantic *robe de style* with beaded and embroidered motifs, she also designed flapper chemises and slinky satin evening gowns.

Lelong, Lucien (1889–1952)

Designer and entrepreneur, Lelong founded the eponymous fashion house in 1918, which became well known for its beautiful fabrics and sophisticated and minimalist dresses and evening wear. In the mid-1920s, he created the style he called 'kineticism', with its flowing lines that were the epitome of elegance in motion.

Lucile, Lady Duff Gordon (1863–1935)

English fashion designer, born Lucy Sutherland. Noted for her luxurious layered and draped garments in soft pastel fabrics, often with sprays of hand-made silk flowers, which became a signature of her work. Best remembered for her work in the performing arts, she costumed stage shows and silent films.

Maison Gripoix

Parisian costume jewellers founded in 1869, known particularly for their glass jewellery. Jeanne Lanvin and Coco Chanel were among their clients.

Mandalian

American manufacturer of mesh bags, founded by Turkish-born Sahatiel Mandalian in 1915.

Mauboussin

French jewellery firm founded in 1827, which produced magnificent Art Deco pieces in the 1920s.

Molyneux, Edward (1891–1974)

British fashion designer who established his Paris fashion house in 1919. His style was simple in the extreme, always refined and sophisticated, but never predictable.

Paquin, Jeanne (1869–1936)
Influential French fashion designer, known for her modern and innovative designs. She pioneered the use of contrasting fabrics such as chiffon with fur, and contrasting colours such as black with pink.

Patou, Jean (1880–1936)
French designer, particularly famous for his high-fashion knitwear designs. His style emphasized a casual and modern elegance.

Perugia, André (1893–1977)
Considered to be the first major shoe designer of the twentieth century, he designed for Paul Poiret and other large fashion houses. He drew inspiration from modern art, industrial design and the Orient.

Poiret, Paul (1879–1944)
French couturier, who established his own house in 1903. He irrevocably changed the feminine form by dispensing with the corset and creating streamlined designs, however fell slightly out of fashion in the 1920s and sold the rights to his business in 1925.

Pringle
Scottish brand of luxury knitwear in cashmere, lambswool and Shetland wool, founded by Robert Pringle in 1815. Their iconic argyle pattern, forever associated with the Duke of Windsor, was developed in the 1920s.

H&M Rayne
English shoemakers, founded in 1889, which produced shoes for theatre productions and major international films, as well as for fashion. Under the direction of Edward Rayne, the company thrived, acquiring three Royal Warrants.

Regny, Jane
French couturier and well-known tennis player, who designed fashions for sport and travel.

Sandoz, Gérard (1902–1988)
Parisian jewellery designer, whose stark, linear style was highly influential.

Schiaparelli, Elsa (1890–1973)
Italian designer whose 'pour le sport' knitwear and trompe l'oeil sweaters stormed the fashion world in the 1920s. A hugely respected creative genius, she is known for her Surrealist designs and collaborations with Salvador Dalí and Jean Cocteau.

Slutzky, Naum (1898–1965)
Ukrainian-born Bauhaus jewellery designer and master goldsmith, whose work is characterized by a simple elegance without ornamentation.

Smedley, John
Innovative British knitwear manufacturer, primarily known in the 1920s as a high-quality manufacturer of underwear made from Sea Island Cotton.

Templier, Raymond (1891–1968)
Jeweller whose work is known for its abstract geometric shapes. He produced some of the most powerful and sophisticated jewellery of the period.

Van Cleef & Arpels
French jewellery, watch and perfume company, founded in 1896. Milestone creations include the first watch with a leather strap in 1923, and a bracelet depicting red and white roses in bloom, made with diamonds, rubies and emeralds in 1925.

Vionnet, Madeleine (1876–1975)
French dressmaker, with a talent for geometry and a revolutionary approach to design. She invented the bias cut and created designs using only one seam. Her designs were often so deconstructed and draped that clients needed instructions in how to put them on.

Whiting & Davis
American manufacturer of mesh bags, which were initially made of sterling silver or vermeil but, as the 1920s wore on, the company began to explore lower-priced alternatives to broaden their customer base. These were made of base metals, often painted with vivid patterns.

Index

Page numbers in *italic* refer to illustration captions.

Acknowledgements

The publishers would like to thank the following sources for their kind permission to reproduce the pictures in this book.

Key: t=Top, b=Bottom, c=Centre, l=Left and r=Right

Page 1 Fiell Archive; **3** Fiell Archive; **4** © Victoria and Albert Museum, London; **5** Northampton Museum & Art Gallery; **6** Getty Images/Hulton Archive; **8** Fiell Archive; **9** Fiell Archive; **10t** Corbis/Bettman; **10c** Carlton Books; **10b** Getty Images/Hulton Archive; **11t** TopFoto.co.uk; **11c** Corbis/Hulton-Deutsch Collection; **11b** Fiell Archive; **12t** Mary Evans Picture Library; **12c** Rex Features/CSU Archives/Everett Collection; **12b** Getty Images/Hulton Archive; **13t** Mary Evans Picture Library; **13c** Mary Evans Picture Library; **13b** Rex Features/Everett Collection; **14t** Getty Images/Hulton Archive; **14c** Mary Evans Picture Library; **14b** Northampton Museum & Art Gallery; **15t** Mary Evans Picture Library; **15c** Northampton Museum & Art Gallery; **15b** Northampton Museum & Art Gallery; **16t** Mary Evans Picture Library/© Illustrated London News Ltd; **16c** Getty Images/Hulton Archive; **16b** Hampshire Museums Service; **17t** Hampshire Museums Service; **17c** Getty Images/Hulton Archive; **17b** Constance Howard Resource & Research Centre in Textiles; **18t** Past Perfect Vintage/www.pastperfectvintage.com/Courtesy Holly Jenkins-Evans; **18m** Getty Images/Hulton Archive; **18b** Past Perfect Vintage/www.pastperfectvintage.com/Courtesy Holly Jenkins-Evans; **19t** Past Perfect Vintage/www.pastperfectvintage.com/Courtesy Holly Jenkins-Evans; **19c** © Victoria and Albert Museum, London; **19b** Past Perfect Vintage/www.pastperfectvintage.com/Courtesy Holly Jenkins-Evans; **20–21** Fiell Archive; **22** Corbis/Condé Nast Archive; **23** Carlton Books; **24** Carlton Books; **25** Carlton Books; **26** Fiell Archive; **27** Carlton Books; **29t&br** Carlton Books; **29bl** Corbis; **31** Carlton Books; **32l** Carlton Books; **32r** Fiell Archive; **33** Carlton Books; **34** Corbis/Historical Picture Archive; **37** Carlton Books; **38–39** Carlton Books; **40** Carlton Books; **41** Getty Images/Hulton Archive; **42** Getty Images/Hulton Archive; **44–45** Carlton Books; **46** Getty Images/Hulton Archive/Brooke; **47** Carlton Books; **48–49** Carlton Books; **50–51** Carlton Books; **52** Getty Images/Hulton Archive; **53** Carlton Books; **54–55** Carlton Books; **57** The Bridgeman Art Library/© Leeds Museums and Galleries (Lotherton Hall) U.K.; **58** © Victoria and Albert Museum, London; **59** Corbis/Bettman; **61** Corbis/Bettman; **62** Corbis/Condé Nast Archive; **63** © Victoria and Albert Museum, London; **64** Corbis/Condé Nast Archive; **66** Corbis/Hulton-Deutsch Collection; **69** Getty Images/Popperfoto; **70** Getty Images/Hulton Archive; **71t** © Victoria and Albert Museum, London; **71c** Northampton Museum & Art Gallery; **71b** Corbis/Hulton-Deutsch Collection; **72t** Getty Images/Hulton Archive; **72b** Mary Evans Picture Library; **73** Getty Images/Hulton Archive; **74** Getty Images/Archive Photos; **75** Getty Images/Hulton Archive; **76** Getty Images/Hulton Archive; **77** Getty Images/Archive Photos; **78** © Victoria and Albert Museum, London; **79** Mary Evans Picture Library/© Illustrated London News Ltd; **80** Corbis; **81** Getty Images/Hulton Archive; **82** Mary Evans Picture Library; **83** Mary Evans Picture Library; **84** Getty Images/Hulton Archive; **85** Corbis/Hulton-Deutsch Collection; **86** Getty Images/Hulton Archive; **87** Musée International de la Chaussure, Romans-sur-Isère-France/Christophe Villard; **88** Getty Images/Roger Viollet; **89** Corbis/Swim Ink 2, LLC; **90** Corbis/Bettman; **91** Musée International de la Chaussure, Romans-sur-Isère-France/Christophe Villard; **92** Musée International de la Chaussure, Romans-sur-Isère-France/Christophe Villard; **93** Mary Evans Picture Library; **94** ©Bata Shoe Museum, Toronto; **95** Corbis/Condé Nast Archive; **96** Corbis/Condé Nast Archive; **97** Carlton Books; **98** Getty Images/Hulton Archive; **99** Getty Images/Hulton Archive; **100** Fiell Archive; **101** Mary Evans Picture Library/© Illustrated London News Ltd; **102** © Victoria and Albert Museum, London; **103** Corbis/Underwood & Underwood; **104** © Victoria and Albert Museum, London; **105** © Victoria and Albert Museum, London; **106** DLM Deutsches Ledermuseum Schuhmuseum Offenbach; **107t** The Art Archive/Collection Dagli Orti; **107b** Getty Images/Liz McAulay; **108** Corbis/Hulton-Deutsch Collection; **109** Mary Evans Picture Library/© Illustrated London News Ltd; **110** Corbis/Underwood & Underwood; **111l** Chanel/Laurent Herail; **111r** TopFoto.co.uk; **112** Hampshire Museums Service; **113t** Hampshire Museums Service; **113b** Mary Evans Picture Library/© Illustrated London News Ltd; **115** Hampshire Museums Service; **116l** © Victoria and Albert Museum, London; **116r** Fiell Archive; **117** Hampshire Museums Service; **118** Corbis/Condé Nast Archive; **120** Corbis/Condé Nast Archive; **121** © Victoria and Albert Museum, London; **122** Mary Evans Picture Library/© Illustrated London News Ltd; **123** Mary Evans Picture Library; **124** © Victoria and Albert Museum, London; **125** © Victoria and Albert Museum, London; **126** © Victoria and Albert Museum, London; **127** The Art Archive/Victoria and Albert Museum London/Eileen Tweedy; **128** Mary Evans Picture Library/© Illustrated London News Ltd; **129** Getty Images/Hulton Archive; **130** © Victoria and Albert Museum, London; **131** Corbis/Condé Nast Archive; **133** The Art Archive; **134** Fiell Archive; **135** Fiell Archive; **136–137** The Art Archive/Collection Dagli Orti.

Every effort has been made to acknowledge correctly and contact the source and/or copyright holder of each picture and Carlton Books Limited apologizes for any unintentional errors or omissions, which will be, corrected in future editions of this book.